SALVATION

God's Instruction on "How to Be Saved"

Includes a full copy
of the Book of Acts
from the Holy Bible

The Book of Salvation—God's Instruction on How to Be Saved
By Fred Beall and Doug Joseph

ISBN: 1453839801
EAN-13:   9781453839805

Contains a copy of the Book of Acts from the Holy Bible (KJV)

Printed in the United States of America.

Azusa StreetRiders, Inc.
P.O. Box 7606
Myrtle Beach, SC 29572

This book may be purchased online at:
www.azusastreetriders.com
www.authorstock.com
and other fine book sellers.

Pastors, churches, bookstores, retailers, and distributors may buy this book at a discount (quantity restrictions may or may not apply for wholesale pricing). For details, contact us at:

Azusa StreetRiders, Inc.
P.O. Box 7606
Myrtle Beach, SC 29572

Phone: (843) 450-6200
Fax: (843) 692-7656
Email: fred.beall@azusastreetriders.com
Web: http://azusastreetriders.com

CONTENTS

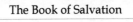

PREFACE

The Holy Bible answers very important questions such as:

- *Is there life after death? (Yes.)*
- *Is there a heaven and hell? (Yes.)*
- *What does it truly take to be saved from sin and escape hell? (See below.)*

Sin means "violation against God's law," Once you start sinning, it gets power over you, and its penalty is eternal damnation. *Salvation* refers to deliverance from both the power of sin and penalty of sin. (This is also referred to as *redemption*.) More on it soon!

The Holy Bible is a *sacred library* containing 66 books that were breathed by God and recorded by holy men of old. [*Holy* = "sacred", *Bible* = "book(s).")] All the books in the Bible are inspired by God, but one of them — *The Book of the Acts of the Apostles* — reveals an important, easy-to-understand summary of how to be saved (how to get in on God's plan for your salvation). That is the primary focus of this study. A full copy of *The Book of Acts* is provided inside this book. First, though, let's talk about the reasons why all of this is so important.

What Happens at Death?

The Bible reveals that at the moment of death each person's eternal soul goes to either *heaven* (and from there to spend eternity with Christ in paradise) or to *hell* (and from there to spend eternity in the lake of fire, trapped with the devil and his fallen angels in torment). Those with Christ will have joy unspeakable for all eternity; no heartache, pain, sickness, disease or sin. In the lake of fire there will be constant pain, torment, and misery.

I'm Already a "Christian." I Don't Need to Read This. Right?

If you consider yourself a Christian then this study is for you. The Bible speaks frequently about "false teachers" (II Peter 2:1) and "other doctrine[s]" (I Timothy 1:3) and strongly indicates that people can be fooled and <u>most</u> will be lost for eternity. The Lord Jesus explained that the majority of those professing themselves to be His followers will be lost, and that only a few of them will be saved (see Matthew 7:13-27). Are you basing your salvation on lies?

Today, about 2,000 years after Jesus Christ walked on this earth, many highly-educated men have twisted the truth about what it takes to be saved. Why would they do so?

Because of not having a love of the truth
(II Thessalonians 2:10). They may have
studied in great seminaries across the
world, sat in awe of well-known teachers,
worn out the pages of Bibles and Bible com-
mentaries in their studies, but yet the Word
of God describes them as "ever learning,
and never able to come to the knowledge of
the truth" (II Timothy 3:7).

This study, <u>The Book of Salvation</u>, **only**
addresses what it takes to "get saved" —
not what it takes to "stay saved." That is
another topic of study for another day.
Nevertheless, do not be fooled by what is
possibly Satan's greatest damnable lie — that
"once you are saved, you are always saved."
Recognize that doctrine for what it is — false
teaching that can send you to hell.

The Bible is Not Just Another Book.
All serious Bible study is based on the belief
that **the entire Bible is the infallible Word
of God without internal contradictions.** If
you think otherwise, it is simply a waste of
your time to go further. God's answers for
your life — regarding questions both earthly
and heavenly — will simply elude your
understanding unless you *first* recognize
that the Bible is your roadmap to blessings
and ultimately to heaven.

If you read and study further, it is assumed that you accept the premise that **the Bible was authored by God Himself**. It is not merely suggestions to consider for "nice ways to live life" or just an historical record of the Jewish people. God used men to pen the words to everlasting life. Even though written thousands of years ago, God's words and instructions are applicable today, and the Scriptures hold the key to eternal life with Christ.

Would a Loving God Send Anyone to Hell?

Over the past fifty years or so, we have witnessed the eradication of "good" and rise of "evil" in society. Sure, there have always been "good" and "bad" people, but social order has steadily deteriorated, which is evidenced by a daily barrage of godless people touting the benefits of a lifestyle that true Christians consider as ungodly. Such defiance against biblical teaching is accompanied by saying, "*a loving God would not allow anyone to go to hell.*"

Twisted scriptures are quoted from pulpits. Politicians compromise biblical truths. Public school teachers and college professors undermine Christian foundations. All this is for the sake of either self-justification or perhaps for fortune and fame. One of the most blatant examples of such twisting, compromising, and undermining involves the homosexual agenda. Homosexual behavior is clearly declared by God to be sinful, yet universal and unquestioning acceptance of this "alternative lifestyle" is demanded by the media, by politicians, and even by many in the clergy. Just imagine: Once-great Christian movements now debate whether gays and lesbians should have the right to be licensed ministers of the gospel in their denominations. Instead of preaching against sin, they now embrace it and let unrepentant, practicing, professed and boastful sinners lead their congregations. The question should be, "Where are they *leading* the sheep (congregation)?"

This same confusion is clearly identifiable in many denominational teachings on the subject of salvation. If they're wrong on the role of homosexuals in the pulpit, **everything** they teach is suspect! Likewise, if they teach a "form of baptism" or a "plan of salvation" that is not consistent with **all** of the Scriptures, then they make their congregation "twofold more the child of hell than [themselves]" (Matthew 23:15).

This Bible study exposes some soul-damning false teachings (II Peter 2:1) brought forth from so-called "Christian" pulpits world-wide. This study is an effort to direct lost souls to Christ so that they might be saved (Matthew 18:11).

This Bible study does not "sugar coat" the Word of God and does not make excuses for false teachings. As Jesus Himself said, "Search the scriptures; for in them ye think ye have eternal life." And as the Apostle Paul wrote, "Though we, or an angel from heaven, preach any other gospel unto you than that which we have preached unto you, let him be accursed" (Galatians 1:8). You are cautioned that there are many different beliefs about what it takes to be saved—how to gain "salvation." Be assured that this study **only** addresses the doctrine (teaching) of the Apostles of the Lord Jesus Christ, from which we are not to be swayed.

All Bible quotations are from the King James Version unless otherwise noted.

May God bless your sincere study and devotion to His Word.

SECTION 1
THE IMPORTANCE OF THE TRUTH IN ACTS

Definitions (<u>Merriam-Webster Dictionary</u>):

Christian:
1. one who professes belief in the teachings of Jesus Christ.

Belief:
1. a state or habit of mind in which trust or confidence is placed in some person or thing.

2. something believed; especially: a tenet or body of tenets held by a group.

3. conviction of the truth of some statement or the reality of some being or phenomenon especially when based on examination of evidence.

Millions of people worldwide profess Christianity. Unfortunately for many of them, their "examination of evidence" lacks depth or understanding, leading them down a path of false security towards damnation on Judgment Day.

The Bible says, "Study to shew thyself approved unto God, a workman that needeth not to be ashamed, rightly dividing the word of truth" (II Timothy 2:15). We can see a contrast between truth & false doctrine, and between truthful teachers & false teachers:

Truthful teachers proclaim (and the truth yields):	By contrast, false teachers and false doctrines yield:
Genuine faith that leads to repentance from sin	Bogus claim that converts should go on living in sin
Genuine faith results in the New Birth experience	No teaching of the New Birth; it does not occur
Full salvation from sin's power & penalty by faith in Jesus	False sense of hope; followers deceived, yet "feel" secure

II Timothy 2:15 says to *study* with the admonition to rightly divide the word of truth. Two quick points:

- *We need to study the Bible.*
- *We must not take the Bible's words out of context. (Do you unknowingly do this? Keep reading. You might be surprised!)*

A serious problem with many self-proclaimed Christians today is that they do not understand the **proper divisions of the Bible** — they do not *rightly divide the word of truth*. The result of that mistake will likely lead their souls to hell — so-called "Christian" souls.

Remember that Jesus said, "Many will say to me in that day, Lord, Lord, have we not prophesied in thy name? and in thy name have cast out devils? and in thy name done many wonderful works? And then will I profess unto them, I never knew you: depart from me, ye that work iniquity" (Matthew 7:22-23). This prophecy of our Lord addresses people who truly *think* of themselves as *saved, believing Christians* or else they would have never prophesied, cast out devils and done many wonderful works in the name of Jesus! On Judgment Day they will learn they only **thought** they were "saved" — they will even argue with Jesus, only to find themselves sentenced to an eternity in the lake of fire.

So-called *believing Christians* who did "wonderful works" will be denied entrance to heaven, and the Bible points out that they will be judged "according to their works" (Revelation 20:12). What did they do wrong?

Their mistake was that they *"received not the love of the truth, that they might be saved"* (II Thessalonians 2:10). Why? Because they did not "rightly divide the word of truth." Don't make their mistake. Accept *the truth* as taught by the Apostles of our Lord Jesus Christ in the Bible. Sadly, this is where most people fall short; they don't want to accept "the truth."

Do you see how important "the truth" is in determining our salvation? It cannot be ignored. What is "the truth"? It is the gospel or doctrine that was taught by the Apostles of Jesus Christ. It is *that* simple — "the truth" is the *Apostles' Doctrine*, or the *Apostolic Doctrine*.

Yet *many* churches claim to teach the Apostles' Doctrine; many claim to have "the truth." No preacher says, "We don't preach truth here." In reality, *Apostolic truth is taught in very few "Christian" pulpits* across the globe. Sadly, over the past 2,000 years, so-called men of God have perverted the Apostles' Doctrine to the point that it is barely recognizable today. False teachings and heresies have and are permeating the hearts and minds of otherwise well-intentioned people. Were it not for these people following false teachers, they might other-

4

wise be found acceptable on Judgment Day, hearing Christ say instead, "Well done, thou good and faithful servant."

Why do they not take advantage of the free salvation provided by Jesus Christ? **They will spend eternity in "outer darkness" where "there shall be weeping and gnashing of teeth" (Matthew 25:30) because they followed a teacher who was not sincere in study of the Bible, and they themselves did not check what their pastor or priest taught against the Word of God—they did not study to show themselves approved and they did not rightly divide the word of truth.** If they had, they would have discovered that their priest or pastor did not teach "the truth" that the Bible insists upon.

Paul and the other Apostles were adamant and unrelenting on preaching of "the truth" to the point that Paul wrote in Galatians 1:8, "But though we, or an angel from heaven, preach any other gospel unto you than that which we have preached unto you, let him be accursed." It should be noted that Paul and **all** the other Apostles taught **only one gospel or doctrine**. They all taught exactly the same message regarding salvation. Around the globe and across the ages, Jesus Christ has but one true church. **There is**

**only one true message of salvation for
which Christ died.**

Concerning salvation, all churches **should**
preach exactly the same things the Apostles
preached. All should preach the same
things about baptism, and all should teach
exactly the same basic truths about how to
live for Christ. Yet, as you know, this is not
so. Even 2,000 years ago Paul recognized
that a perverted or altered gospel, word, or
doctrine was infiltrating churches and pulpits, the followers of which had departed
from true salvation.

So, how do we know what is *the truth* of
which the Apostle Paul spoke, and how do
we determine what church preaches *the
truth*? Before we go any further, remember
that Jesus said in Mark 10:15, "Verily I say
unto you, Whosoever shall not receive the
kingdom of God as a little child, he shall not
enter therein." The simplicity of this statement pinpoints the difficulty most adults
have in receiving God's Word. Paul wrote
in II Timothy 3:7 of men that were "ever
learning, and never able to come to the
knowledge of *the truth*." Little children
gladly believe, yet adults find "…some
things hard to be understood, which they
that are unlearned and unstable wrest, as

they do also the other scriptures, unto their own destruction" (II Peter 3:16). In other words, they wrestle with the Scriptures to the point that they do not accept "the truth" and are eventually lost to the flames of hell.

Remember, the point of this Bible study, The Book of Salvation, is to find what the Word of God says about "how to be saved." We are not to go by any contrary opinions of men, whether preacher, priest, pastor, mom, dad, grandma, or grandpa. **The Word of God — the Bible — is what matters.** The importance of the Bible in comparison to man's ideas is underscored in Romans 3:4 where Paul forcefully exhorted the Roman church to "let God be true, but every man a liar." Keeping this in mind, **do not let it matter** how "invested" you are in your church. So what if:

- you know every person in the church and they are all good people
- you're on the Deacon Board
- your granddaddy built the church
- all your children were baptized there
- your parents are buried in the cemetery behind the church building
- you teach Sunday School in your church

If the church you currently attend is not a place where "the truth" is taught, you need to leave it and find a church where "the truth" is not only taught, but *emphasized.* "Truth" will be discussed further as this Bible study progresses. Your salvation is at stake! Will it be Heaven or hell for you? Remember what the Apostle Paul wrote: "Study to shew thyself approved unto God, a workman that needeth not to be ashamed, rightly dividing the word of truth."

HOW TO RIGHTLY DIVIDE GOD'S WORD:

Context

To rightly divide the word of truth, **we need to notice to whom a scripture was initially written and for what purpose it was written**. This pertains to what is called *context*. It is *this* basic, just like Jesus said about receiving the kingdom of God as a little child. We do not need to wrestle the Scriptures to our own self destruction. By taking note of the context we can place (divide) the Scriptures into some basic categories or divisions for proper application in our lives. If we do so *properly*, we are then "rightly dividing the word of truth," and this effort is also causing us to study to show ourselves approved unto God.

There are two main divisions:
The Old Testament and the New Testament.

The **Old Testament** tells about the time before Jesus came, spanning from the beginning of Creation until about 400 years before the birth of Jesus. It includes several types of books:

- The Law (first five books; which were written by Moses)
- Books of Jewish History
- Wisdom, poetry, and song
- Books of Prophecy

The **New Testament** is focused on the Church Age, spanning from the time when Jesus was born and onward. It includes the first several decades of the Church's history. It has these categories:

- Gospels (first four books - which are about Jesus' life, ministry & death)
- One book of Church History (Acts)
- Epistles (Letters to those already saved according to the truth in Acts)
- One book of Prophecy (the Book of Revelation)

In the Old Testament ages, God's people could be saved by faith in Him. From the time of Abraham (the first Jew) onward, saving faith was demonstrated by being (or becoming) Jewish. (People of other nations could be saved, but they were to become Jewish to be saved.) Their salvation was all dependent on the then-future death of Jesus to finally pay for their sins in full. Old Testament prophets predicted the coming of a New Covenant age (the Church Age) when God's salvation would be available to all nations without anyone needing to become Jewish in order to be saved. The coming Jewish Messiah (Jesus the Christ) was predicted to provide salvation that would be available to all. Ever since the death, burial and resurrection of Jesus, humanity has lived during that predicted New Covenant age. The New Testament pertains to the New Covenant (Church Age), so we will focus on the New Testament in our study of "what it takes to be saved." Although much can be gleaned from the Old Testament and applied to our lives today, "how to be saved" is the purpose of this Bible study, so we will focus on the New Testament. In fact, we will focus on the path to salvation found in the New Testament, particularly the Book of Acts.

The New Testament has four divisions:

1. **The Gospels** (the books of Matthew, Mark, Luke, and John)
2. **The Book of Acts**, also called **The Acts of the Apostles** (the only biblical book of church history)
3. **The Epistles** (the books spanning from Romans through Jude; letters from the Apostles to churches/individuals)
4. **The Book of Revelation**

Remember: The Bible was authored by God. He used men to pen the words. This is akin to a secretary taking dictation. The secretary may not understand what he/she is writing, yet they write it anyway. The Bible's writers recorded what God instructed them to write. Keep this in mind. Let's talk a little more about the New Testament's divisions:

1. **The Gospels** are basically the recorded observations about the life of Jesus by four men: Matthew, Mark, Luke, and John. Although many of the same events are recorded in two or more of the gospels, the reason for the multiple witnesses is to help in our understanding of the life of Christ on earth. They cover the life, preaching, teaching, and actions of Jesus Christ from his birth to

around the time of His ascension into heaven following His death, burial and resurrection.

2. **The Book of Acts** (or **The Acts of the Apostles**) is a historical narrative of the authentic deeds — words, sayings, teachings, and physical actions — of the Apostles of Jesus Christ.

Definition of **Apostle:**
one of an authoritative New Testament group sent out to preach the gospel and made up especially of Christ's original disciples and Paul.

Notes of Interest: *One of Jesus' original twelve disciples, Judas Iscariot, chose to betray the Lord, and Judas later hung himself in his overwhelming guilt. He was replaced by Matthias through a vote of the remaining eleven disciples. The ascended Lord appointed an anti-Christian Jew, named Saul, to be an Apostle (saving & renaming him Paul). After Jesus' ascension, the term **Apostle** replaced **Disciple** in describing these men. The Lord Jesus entrusted His truth in these men, via His teachings, calling, and indwelling Spirit.*

In the God-inspired Book of Acts we read about the words, deeds, and teachings of the Apostles as they began to evangelize a lost world. We read about the places where they preached and founded new churches (all of which had the same essential doctrine regarding salvation), the turmoil that they caused among idol worshippers, and the rejection they faced for preaching about Jesus. We learn the formula they used when they baptized new converts (it was in Jesus name), and we read of a supernatural event when new converts were filled with the Holy Spirit. **It is in the Book of Acts that we can find out "how to be saved" and we can see the fact that salvation is available to all.**

3. **The Epistles** are the books of the New Testament from Romans through Jude—21 books altogether. They are God-inspired letters to churches or individuals. **Take note that each of these epistles were written to people who had already obeyed the things preached in the Book of Acts to be saved.** Without exception, these letters were written to people or congregations that had already obeyed the gospel and

had enjoyed the "new birth" experience unto salvation. The purpose of these epistles was to teach Christians who were "already saved" about how to "stay saved" — to help them overcome the trials of life and live in a manner that would grow them in Christ. **We must go to the Book of Acts, not the epistles, in order to read the biblical, historical record of the Apostles' teachings to lost souls about an initial conversion and new birth into the Church. The epistles corroborate the Book of Acts, but they do not contradict it or supercede its teachings about conversion.**

4. **The Book of Revelation** is essentially a prophecy book that reveals Jesus in His true glory and tells of events yet to come. The author, John, was personally visited by Jesus Christ, who revealed many things about the end of the age.

Noting the four divisions of the New Testament cited above, we can now more easily see how to "rightly divide the word of truth" in order to be saved.

A very important passage in the gospels is found in John 17:17-20. In a portion of Jesus' prayer, prior to His death on the cross, He prayed for the disciples that He had "sent into the world." In verse 20, our Lord said, "Neither pray I for these alone, but for them also which shall believe on me through their word." Note that we are to believe on the Lord *through their word* — the word of the Apostles. The Book of Acts contains very important details about their word — what they preached and taught to lost souls about conversion to Christianity.

To further emphasize the importance of the Apostles' words, in Matthew 16:18-19, Jesus told Peter (one of His disciples and one of the future Apostles) that upon "*this rock*" (the revelation of who Jesus is) the Lord would build His church and the gates of hell shall not prevail against it. In verse 19, Jesus said to Peter, "And I will give unto thee (Peter) the keys of the kingdom of heaven: and whatsoever thou (Peter) shalt bind on earth shall be bound in heaven: and whatsoever thou (Peter) shalt loose on earth shall be loosed in heaven." Therefore it is critically important that we pay close attention to what Peter said in the only biblical history book of the first-century church; the only book where Peter's words to lost souls are recorded verbatim — The Book of Acts.

The sole purpose of this Bible study is to show exactly what God wants us to do to *initially* "be saved." Life beyond that experience is the topic of another study. It is not the purpose of this study to help one live an "overcoming" life after doing what it takes to "be saved." **The express purpose of this study is to explain in child-like simplicity what God wants us to do to "be saved."**

According to Jesus Christ, one must be born again to see the kingdom of God (John 3:3). How? Jesus taught that "Except a man be born of **water** and of the **Spirit**, he cannot enter into the kingdom of God" (John 3:5). In the Book of Acts, we can see exactly what was meant by Jesus with reference to these two aspects (water and Spirit) of the "new birth" of which He spoke. The Apostles make it very clear: Water baptism in Jesus name and the baptism of the Holy Spirit.

Since the Book of Acts is the place to easily see what one must do to "be saved," the remainder of this study will concentrate on the Book of Acts. In fact, it is copied verbatim (King James Version) over the next few pages. To help explain the steps necessary to "be saved" some comments about the Scriptures are provided in a side area reserved for notes.

After you have obeyed the things that the Apostles tell us to do to "be saved" — once you have experienced the "new birth" (being born of the water and of the Spirit, see John 3:3-5), then all the later books will have application in your life. *But until that time, reading the epistles will be like reading someone else's mail.* To read about how to "stay saved" a saved person should go to the epistles (such as the Book of Romans, etc), but to read about how to "get saved" a lost person should obey the Book of Acts. Consider this metaphor: To learn about a car's maintenance schedule you would not go to its warranty card, and to learn about its warranty you would not go to its maintenance guide. Remember to "rightly divide the word of truth." The epistles (such as the Book of Romans, etc) were written to churches that had **already been born again. They had already obeyed the steps to "be saved,"** as found in the Book of Acts.

Be aware in advance that those who are vested in a false doctrine will likely disagree with studying the Book of Acts to find out how to "be saved." They may rebuke this writer, claiming instead that the Book of Acts will only cause "confusion" for people considering conversion to Christianity.

In other words, studying the Bible, specifically the Book of Acts, results in an Apostolic approach that doesn't match what they teach, and this therefore causes "confusion." Actually, it is their teachings that are contrary to God's Word that cause confusion. Such opponents of truth seek to blur your focus away from the Book of Acts, taking you to other books instead because their teachings do not accord with the words of the Apostles recorded in Acts. Go instead with the Book of Acts! Remember, the original Apostles had already had their understanding opened by the Lord Jesus Christ (see Luke 24:45). In any contradiction between the Apostles and anyone else, siding with the Apostles is the right way to side with what Jesus wants for your life.

Some opponents of truth fight against the teachings in the Book of Acts because they lack understanding; they lack the revelation of how to *rightly divide the word of truth*. In Luke 24:44-49, after Jesus was resurrected, He opened "their (the Apostles') understanding that they might understand the scriptures" and instructed them, showing how that "repentance and remission of sins should be preached in his name among all nations, beginning at Jerusalem" (v. 47).

Remember that the Apostles' teaching, preaching, and actions were recorded for our use today, right in the Book of Acts. Apostle Paul warned, "But though we, or an angel from heaven, preach any other gospel unto you than that which we have preached unto you, let him be accursed." (Galatians 1:8). What they preached is found in the Book of Acts. It is unwise to depart from the plan of salvation found in the Book of Acts!

From this point forward, we will study the Book of Acts, an extremely important part of the Bible, God's Book of Salvation.

Section 2
The Book of Acts:
Its Setting & Contents

To provide a setting for *The Book of Acts*, consider that it was written by Luke (the same Luke who wrote the gospel bearing his name). Acts is essentially a sequel to his gospel—a sequel in which Luke continued his recording of historical events. His gospel recorded events prior to the Church Age, and Acts recorded the beginning of the Church Age and events during its first few decades.

Jesus had lived His earthly life, ministering for about three and a half years in the presence of the disciples and many other witnesses. He was crucified (a type of execution) and was buried, and then He rose from the dead after the third day.

The general time period covered by Acts began about six weeks after the resurrection of Jesus from the dead, and about ten days prior to the Day of Pentecost, which was an annual Jewish feast (one of several important feasts the Jews had been celebrating for generations according to God's command). Those feasts are a study unto themselves.

It is suggested that you read the Book of Acts through from start to finish, noting the comments concerning repentance, water baptism, Holy Ghost baptism, the formation of churches in various cities, and the introductions of several important biblical figures. After reading it through completely, then a slower, more detailed, more thorough reading is recommended, concentrating the second time on the areas where comments have been offered.

The Book of Acts
From the Holy Bible

Acts Chapter 1

1 The former treatise have I made, O Theophilus, of all that Jesus began both to do and teach,

2 Until the day in which he was taken up, after that he through the Holy Ghost had given commandments unto the apostles whom he had chosen:

3 To whom also he shewed himself alive after his passion by many infallible proofs, being seen of them forty days, and speaking of the things pertaining to the kingdom of God:

4 And, being assembled together with them, commanded them that they should not depart from Jerusalem, but wait for the promise of the Father, which, saith he, ye have heard of me.

5 For John truly baptized with water; but ye shall be baptized with the Holy Ghost not many days hence.

6 When they therefore were come together, they asked of him, saying, Lord, wilt thou at this time

1:1: "former treatise" is the Gospel of Luke, written prior to Acts.

restore again the kingdom to Israel?

7 And he said unto them, It is not for you to know the times or the seasons, which the Father hath put in his own power.

8 But ye shall receive power, after that the Holy Ghost is come upon you: and ye shall be witnesses unto me both in Jerusalem, and in all Judaea, and in Samaria, and unto the uttermost part of the earth.

9 And when he had spoken these things, while they beheld, he was taken up; and a cloud received him out of their sight.

10 And while they looked stedfastly toward heaven as he went up, behold, two men stood by them in white apparel;

11 Which also said, Ye men of Galilee, why stand ye gazing up into heaven? this same Jesus, which is taken up from you into heaven, shall so come in like manner as ye have seen him go into heaven.

12 Then returned they unto Jerusalem from the mount called Olivet, which is from Jerusalem a sabbath day's journey.

13 And when they were come in, they went up into an upper room, where abode both Peter, and James, and John, and Andrew,

Philip, and Thomas, Bartholomew, and Matthew, James the son of Alphaeus, and Simon Zelotes, and Judas the brother of James.

14 These all continued with one accord in prayer and supplication, with the women, and Mary the mother of Jesus, and with his brethren.

15 And in those days Peter stood up in the midst of the disciples, and said, (the number of names together were about an hundred and twenty,)

16 Men and brethren, this scripture must needs have been fulfilled, which the Holy Ghost by the mouth of David spake before concerning Judas, which was guide to them that took Jesus.

17 For he was numbered with us, and had obtained part of this ministry.

18 Now this man purchased a field with the reward of iniquity; and falling headlong, he burst asunder in the midst, and all his bowels gushed out.

19 And it was known unto all the dwellers at Jerusalem; insomuch as that field is called in their proper tongue, Aceldama, that is to say, The field of blood.

Notes:

1:14: Mary, Jesus' mother, was in the upper room praying. While her role in God's plan is worthy of respect, she is not deity and should not be treated as such. Also note they were all in prayer regarding the same things.

Notes:

20 For it is written in the book of Psalms, Let his habitation be desolate, and let no man dwell therein: and his bishoprick let another take.

21 Wherefore of these men which have companied with us all the time that the Lord Jesus went in and out among us,

22 Beginning from the baptism of John, unto that same day that he was taken up from us, must one be ordained to be a witness with us of his resurrection.

23 And they appointed two, Joseph called Barsabas, who was surnamed Justus, and Matthias.

24 And they prayed, and said, Thou, Lord, which knowest the hearts of all men, shew whether of these two thou hast chosen,

25 That he may take part of this ministry and apostleship, from which Judas by transgression fell, that he might go to his own place.

26 And they gave forth their lots; and the lot fell upon Matthias; and he was numbered with the eleven apostles.

1:26: Matthias was selected to replace Judas Iscariot, to be counted among the twelve Apostles.

Acts Chapter 2

1 And when the day of Pentecost was fully come, they were all with one accord in one place.

2 And suddenly there came a sound from heaven as of a rushing mighty wind, and it filled all the house where they were sitting.

3 And there appeared unto them cloven tongues like as of fire, and it sat upon each of them.

4 And they were all filled with the Holy Ghost, and began to speak with other tongues, as the Spirit gave them utterance.

5 And there were dwelling at Jerusalem Jews, devout men, out of every nation under heaven.

6 Now when this was noised abroad, the multitude came together, and were confounded, because that every man heard them speak in his own language.

7 And they were all amazed and marvelled, saying one to another, Behold, are not all these which speak Galilaeans?

8 And how hear we every man in our own tongue, wherein we were born?

9 Parthians, and Medes, and Elamites, and the dwellers in Mesopotamia, and in Judaea, and Cappadocia, in Pontus, and Asia,

10 Phrygia, and Pamphylia, in Egypt, and in the parts of Libya about Cyrene, and strangers of

Notes:

2:1-4: This is the first record-ed instance of the long foretold New Covenant baptism of the Holy Ghost. There was an initial, physical evidence, or sign, of speak-ing with other tongues (other languages) as the Spirit of God directed, cf. Acts 10:44-46, 19:6.

Notes:

2:14: The other Apostles stood with Peter, indicating agreement with the message—all the Apostles were in unity. The Lord Jesus had previously told Peter that what he bound on earth would be bound in heaven and what he loosed on earth would be loosed in heaven (Mat.16:19).

2:16-18: Peter explained that this experience (including its evidence) was the outpouring of the Spirit (Holy Ghost) that had been prophesied back in the Old Testament (see Joel 2:28-29).It was also foretold by the Lord Jesus (see John 14:26).

Rome, Jews and proselytes,

11 Cretes and Arabians, we do hear them speak in our tongues the wonderful works of God.

12 And they were all amazed, and were in doubt, saying one to another, What meaneth this?

13 Others mocking said, These men are full of new wine.

14 But Peter, standing up with the eleven, lifted up his voice, and said unto them, Ye men of Judaea, and all ye that dwell at Jerusalem, be this known unto you, and hearken to my words:

15 For these are not drunken, as ye suppose, seeing it is but the third hour of the day.

16 But this is that which was spoken by the prophet Joel;

17 And it shall come to pass in the last days, saith God,I will pour out of my Spirit upon all flesh: and your sons and your daughters shall prophesy, and your young men shall see visions, and your old men shall dream dreams:

18 And on my servants and on my handmaidens I will pour out in those days of my Spirit; and they shall prophesy:

19 And I will shew wonders in heaven above, and signs in the

earth beneath; blood, and fire, and vapour of smoke:

20 The sun shall be turned into darkness, and the moon into blood, before that great and notable day of the Lord come:

21 And it shall come to pass, that whosoever shall call on the name of the Lord shall be saved.

22 Ye men of Israel, hear these words; Jesus of Nazareth, a man approved of God among you by miracles and wonders and signs, which God did by him in the midst of you, as ye yourselves also know:

23 Him, being delivered by the determinate counsel and fore-knowledge of God, ye have taken, and by wicked hands have crucified and slain:

24 Whom God hath raised up, having loosed the pains of death: because it was not possible that he should be holden of it.

25 For David speaketh concerning him, I foresaw the Lord always before my face, for he is on my right hand, that I should not be moved:

26 Therefore did my heart rejoice, and my tongue was glad; moreover also my flesh shall rest in hope:

Notes:

2:21: In the New Covenant, calling on the Lord's name includes invoking Jesus' name in baptism (see Acts 2:38, 8:16, 10:48, 22:16). Bible history shows a pattern instituted by God, of having His name invoked over those entering into a covenant relationship with Him; those who pledge to follow His teachings & instructions.

Notes:

27 Because thou wilt not leave my soul in hell, neither wilt thou suffer thine Holy One to see corruption.

28 Thou hast made known to me the ways of life; thou shalt make me full of joy with thy countenance.

29 Men and brethren, let me freely speak unto you of the patriarch David, that he is both dead and buried, and his sepulchre is with us unto this day.

30 Therefore being a prophet, and knowing that God had sworn with an oath to him, that of the fruit of his loins, according to the flesh, he would raise up Christ to sit on his throne;

31 He seeing this before spake of the resurrection of Christ, that his soul was not left in hell, neither his flesh did see corruption.

32 This Jesus hath God raised up, whereof we all are witnesses.

33 Therefore being by the right hand of God exalted, and having received of the Father the promise of the Holy Ghost, he hath shed forth this, which ye now see and hear.

34 For David is not ascended into the heavens: but he saith himself, The LORD said unto my Lord,

Sit thou on my right hand,

35 Until I make thy foes thy footstool.

36 Therefore let all the house of Israel know assuredly, that God hath made that same Jesus, whom ye have crucified, both Lord and Christ.

37 Now when they heard this, they were pricked in their heart, and said unto Peter and to the rest of the apostles, Men and brethren, what shall we do?

38 Then Peter said unto them, Repent, and be baptized every one of you in the name of Jesus Christ for the remission of sins, and ye shall receive the gift of the Holy Ghost.

39 For the promise is unto you, and to your children, and to all that are afar off, even as many as the Lord our God shall call.

40 And with many other words did he testify and exhort, saying, Save

Notes:

2:37: *"What shall we do?"* is no doubt the most important question ever asked. They knew they were lost, and they asked what they should do! The answer was given in v. 38. It is still the correct answer today.

2:38: Three steps are to be obeyed: (1) Repent (turn away from sin), (2) Be water baptized in Jesus name, (3) Receive the gift of the Holy Ghost. (See also: Mark 16:17, Acts 2:4, 10:44-46, 19:6.) This same teaching (repentance and New Birth via water and Spirit) was commanded by the Apostles all through Acts, taught by Jesus (Luke 13:3-5, John 3:3-5), and is corroborated in the epistles.

2:39: Some falsely teach that Holy Spirit baptism is not for today, but this verse teaches otherwise. If God still calls people, then the promise is still available. This promise is applicable to us. Its power is not diminished.

Notes:

2:41: *gladly:* This seems to indicate there were others who did not receive the word and were not baptized. The obedient ones saved themselves from their corrupt ("untoward") generation (v. 40) by gladly acting upon (obeying) Peter's words given in Acts 2:38.

2:42: Yet another indication of the importance of the Apostles' doctrine. Throughout the epistles, the importance of the Apostles' doctrine is further supported.

yourselves from this untoward generation.

41 Then they that gladly received his word were baptized: and the same day there were added unto them about three thousand souls.

42 And they continued stedfastly in the apostles' doctrine and fellowship, and in breaking of bread, and in prayers.

43 And fear came upon every soul: and many wonders and signs were done by the apostles.

44 And all that believed were together, and had all things common;

45 And sold their possessions and goods, and parted them to all men, as every man had need.

46 And they, continuing daily with one accord in the temple, and breaking bread from house to house, did eat their meat with gladness and singleness of heart,

47 Praising God, and having favour with all the people. And the Lord added to the church daily such as should be saved.

Acts Chapter 3

1 Now Peter and John went up together into the temple at the hour of prayer, being the ninth hour.

Notes:

2 And a certain man lame from his mother's womb was carried, whom they laid daily at the gate of the temple which is called Beautiful, to ask alms of them that entered into the temple;

3 Who seeing Peter and John about to go into the temple asked an alms.

4 And Peter, fastening his eyes upon him with John, said, Look on us.

5 And he gave heed unto them, expecting to receive something of them.

6 Then Peter said, Silver and gold have I none; but such as I have give I thee: In the name of Jesus Christ of Nazareth rise up and walk.

7 And he took him by the right hand, and lifted him up: and immediately his feet and ankle bones received strength.

8 And he leaping up stood, and walked, and entered with them into the temple, walking, and leaping, and praising God.

9 And all the people saw him walking and praising God:

10 And they knew that it was he which sat for alms at the Beautiful gate of the temple: and they were

3:8: This is the first recorded miracle done by one of the Apostles, as promised by Jesus (Mark 16:18).

filled with wonder and amazement at that which had happened unto him.

11 And as the lame man which was healed held Peter and John, all the people ran together unto them in the porch that is called Solomon's, greatly wondering.

12 And when Peter saw it, he answered unto the people, Ye men of Israel, why marvel ye at this? or why look ye so earnestly on us, as though by our own power or holiness we had made this man to walk?

13 The God of Abraham, and of Isaac, and of Jacob, the God of our fathers, hath glorified his Son Jesus; whom ye delivered up, and denied him in the presence of Pilate, when he was determined to let him go.

14 But ye denied the Holy One and the Just, and desired a murderer to be granted unto you;

15 And killed the Prince of life, whom God hath raised from the dead; whereof we are witnesses.

16 And his name through faith in his name hath made this man strong, whom ye see and know: yea, the faith which is by him hath given him this perfect soundness in the presence of you all.

17 And now, brethren, I wot that through ignorance ye did it, as did also your rulers.

18 But those things, which God before had shewed by the mouth of all his prophets, that Christ should suffer, he hath so fulfilled.

19 Repent ye therefore, and be converted, that your sins may be blotted out, when the times of refreshing shall come from the presence of the Lord;

20 And he shall send Jesus Christ, which before was preached unto you:

21 Whom the heaven must receive until the times of restitution of all things, which God hath spoken by the mouth of all his holy prophets since the world began.

22 For Moses truly said unto the fathers, A prophet shall the Lord your God raise up unto you of your brethren, like unto me; him shall ye hear in all things whatsoever he shall say unto you.

23 And it shall come to pass, that every soul, which will not hear that prophet, shall be destroyed from among the people.

24 Yea, and all the prophets from Samuel and those that follow after, as many as have spoken, have

Notes:

Notes:

likewise foretold of these days.

25 Ye are the children of the prophets, and of the covenant which God made with our fathers, saying unto Abraham, And in thy seed shall all the kindreds of the earth be blessed.

26 Unto you first God, having raised up his Son Jesus, sent him to bless you, in turning away every one of you from his iniquities.

Acts Chapter 4

1 And as they spake unto the people, the priests, and the captain of the temple, and the Sadducees, came upon them,

2 Being grieved that they taught the people, and preached through Jesus the resurrection from the dead.

4:3: They were arrested and jailed for preaching the gospel and for performing a miracle in Jesus name.

3 And they laid hands on them, and put them in hold unto the next day: for it was now eventide.

4 Howbeit many of them which heard the word believed; and the number of the men was about five thousand.

5 And it came to pass on the morrow, that their rulers, and elders, and scribes,

6 And Annas the high priest, and Caiaphas, and John, and

Notes:

Alexander, and as many as were of the kindred of the high priest, were gathered together at Jerusalem.

7   And when they had set them in the midst, they asked, By what power, or by what name, have ye done this?

8   Then Peter, filled with the Holy Ghost, said unto them, Ye rulers of the people, and elders of Israel,

9   If we this day be examined of the good deed done to the impotent man, by what means he is made whole;

10   Be it known unto you all, and to all the people of Israel, that by the name of Jesus Christ of Nazareth, whom ye crucified, whom God raised from the dead, even by him doth this man stand here before you whole.

11   This is the stone which was set at nought of you builders, which is become the head of the corner.

12   Neither is there salvation in any other: for there is none other name under heaven given among men, whereby we must be saved.

4:12: Only by Jesus (through His name) can we be saved.

13   Now when they saw the boldness of Peter and John, and perceived that they were unlearned and

Notes:

ignorant men, they marvelled; and they took knowledge of them, that they had been with Jesus.

14 And beholding the man which was healed standing with them, they could say nothing against it.

15 But when they had commanded them to go aside out of the council, they conferred among themselves,

16 Saying, What shall we do to these men? for that indeed a notable miracle hath been done by them is manifest to all them that dwell in Jerusalem; and we cannot deny it.

17 But that it spread no further among the people, let us straitly threaten them, that they speak henceforth to no man in this name.

4:17-19: The Apostles were ordered by the authorities to not speak or teach in Jesus name. They obeyed God, not man.

18 And they called them, and commanded them not to speak at all nor teach in the name of Jesus.

19 But Peter and John answered and said unto them, Whether it be right in the sight of God to hearken unto you more than unto God, judge ye.

20 For we cannot but speak the things which we have seen and heard.

21 So when they had further threatened them, they let them go, finding nothing how they might

Notes:

punish them, because of the people: for all men glorified God for that which was done.

22 For the man was above forty years old, on whom this miracle of healing was shewed.

23 And being let go, they went to their own company, and reported all that the chief priests and elders had said unto them.

24 And when they heard that, they lifted up their voice to God with one accord, and said, Lord, thou art God, which hast made heaven, and earth, and the sea, and all that in them is:

25 Who by the mouth of thy servant David hast said, Why did the heathen rage, and the people imagine vain things?

26 The kings of the earth stood up, and the rulers were gathered together against the Lord, and against his Christ.

27 For of a truth against thy holy child Jesus, whom thou hast anointed, both Herod, and Pontius Pilate, with the Gentiles, and the people of Israel, were gathered together,

28 For to do whatsoever thy hand and thy counsel determined before to be done.

29 And now, Lord, behold their

Notes:

4:31: *filled:* It seems these were refilled. (They were initially filled with the Spirit in Acts chapter 2, with the evidence of speaking in other tongues.)

threatenings: and grant unto thy servants, that with all boldness they may speak thy word,

30 By stretching forth thine hand to heal; and that signs and wonders may be done by the name of thy holy child Jesus.

31 And when they had prayed, the place was shaken where they were assembled together; and they were all filled with the Holy Ghost, and they spake the word of God with boldness.

32 And the multitude of them that believed were of one heart and of one soul: neither said any of them that ought of the things which he possessed was his own; but they had all things common.

33 And with great power gave the apostles witness of the resurrection of the Lord Jesus: and great grace was upon them all.

34 Neither was there any among them that lacked: for as many as were possessors of lands or houses sold them, and brought the prices of the things that were sold,

35 And laid them down at the apostles' feet: and distribution was made unto every man according as he had need.

36 And Joses, who by the apos-

tles was surnamed Barnabas, (which is, being interpreted, The son of consolation,) a Levite, and of the country of Cyprus,

37 Having land, sold it, and brought the money, and laid it at the apostles' feet.

Acts Chapter 5

1 But a certain man named Ananias, with Sapphira his wife, sold a possession,

2 And kept back part of the price, his wife also being privy to it, and brought a certain part, and laid it at the apostles' feet.

3 But Peter said, Ananias, why hath Satan filled thine heart to lie to the Holy Ghost, and to keep back part of the price of the land?

4 Whiles it remained, was it not thine own? and after it was sold, was it not in thine own power? why hast thou conceived this thing in thine heart? thou hast not lied unto men, but unto God.

5 And Ananias hearing these words fell down, and gave up the ghost: and great fear came on all them that heard these things.

6 And the young men arose, wound him up, and carried him out, and buried him.

7 And it was about the space of three hours after, when his wife, not knowing what was done, came in.

8 And Peter answered unto her, Tell me whether ye sold the land for so much? And she said, Yea, for so much.

9 Then Peter said unto her, How is it that ye have agreed together to tempt the Spirit of the Lord? behold, the feet of them which have buried thy husband are at the door, and shall carry thee out.

10 Then fell she down straightway at his feet, and yielded up the ghost: and the young men came in, and found her dead, and, carrying her forth, buried her by her husband.

11 And great fear came upon all the church, and upon as many as heard these things.

12 And by the hands of the apostles were many signs and wonders wrought among the people; (and they were all with one accord in Solomon's porch.

13 And of the rest durst no man join himself to them: but the people magnified them.

14 And believers were the more added to the Lord, multitudes both

Notes:

of men and women.)

15 Insomuch that they brought forth the sick into the streets, and laid them on beds and couches, that at the least the shadow of Peter passing by might overshadow some of them.

16 There came also a multitude out of the cities round about unto Jerusalem, bringing sick folks, and them which were vexed with unclean spirits: and they were healed every one.

5:16: Miracles of God were occurring... "and they were healed every one."

17 Then the high priest rose up, and all they that were with him, (which is the sect of the Sadducees,) and were filled with indignation,

18 And laid their hands on the apostles, and put them in the common prison.

5:18: They were again imprisoned for preaching and for the miracles.

19 But the angel of the Lord by night opened the prison doors, and brought them forth, and said,

20 Go, stand and speak in the temple to the people all the words of this life.

5:19: An angel opened the prison and released them.

21 And when they heard that, they entered into the temple early in the morning, and taught. But the high priest came, and they that were with him, and called the council together, and all the senate of the children of Israel and sent to the

Notes:

prison to have them brought.

22 But when the officers came, and found them not in the prison, they returned, and told,

23 Saying, The prison truly found we shut with all safety, and the keepers standing without before the doors: but when we had opened, we found no man within.

24 Now when the high priest and the captain of the temple and the chief priests heard these things, they doubted of them whereunto this would grow.

25 Then came one and told them, saying, Behold, the men whom ye put in prison are standing in the temple, and teaching the people.

26 Then went the captain with the officers, and brought them without violence: for they feared the people, lest they should have been stoned.

27 And when they had brought them, they set them before the council: and the high priest asked them,

28 Saying, Did not we straitly command you that ye should not teach in this name? and, behold, ye have filled Jerusalem with your doctrine, and intend to bring this man's blood upon us.

29 Then Peter and the other apostles answered and said, We ought to obey God rather than men.

30 The God of our fathers raised up Jesus, whom ye slew and hanged on a tree.

31 Him hath God exalted with his right hand to be a Prince and a Saviour, for to give repentance to Israel, and forgiveness of sins.

32 And we are his witnesses of these things; and so is also the Holy Ghost, whom God hath given to them that obey him.

33 When they heard that, they were cut to the heart, and took counsel to slay them.

34 Then stood there up one in the council, a Pharisee, named Gamaliel, a doctor of the law, had in reputation among all the people, and commanded to put the apostles forth a little space;

35 And said unto them, Ye men of Israel, take heed to yourselves what ye intend to do as touching these men.

36 For before these days rose up Theudas, boasting himself to be somebody; to whom a number of men, about four hundred, joined themselves: who was slain; and all,

Notes:

5:29: Peter's statement, "we ought to obey God rather than men" is especially applicable today when seeking salvation. We should obey the Bible, not any contrary doctrines of men.

5:32: Notice that the Holy Ghost is given to them that obey Him.

Notes:

5:40: Note that persecution of the church was present because of the name of Jesus. However, since the Lord was involved in building His church, persecution could not stop what was happening (cf. vv. 33-39).

5:41: Are you willing to suffer shame for Jesus name, as were the Apostles? Today, many mock and ridicule those of the name, those who believe in baptism in Jesus name.

5:42: Despite the persecution, the Apostles continued to preach the truth of Jesus. The same should be done today. We have no excuses.

as many as obeyed him, were scattered, and brought to nought.

37 After this man rose up Judas of Galilee in the days of the taxing, and drew away much people after him: he also perished; and all, even as many as obeyed him, were dispersed.

38 And now I say unto you, Refrain from these men, and let them alone: for if this counsel or this work be of men, it will come to nought:

39 But if it be of God, ye cannot overthrow it; lest haply ye be found even to fight against God.

40 And to him they agreed: and when they had called the apostles, and beaten them, they commanded that they should not speak in the name of Jesus, and let them go.

41 And they departed from the presence of the council, rejoicing that they were counted worthy to suffer shame for his name.

42 And daily in the temple, and in every house, they ceased not to teach and preach Jesus Christ.

Acts Chapter 6

1 And in those days, when the number of the disciples was multiplied, there arose a murmuring of the Grecians against the Hebrews, because their widows were neglected in the daily ministration.

2 Then the twelve called the multitude of the disciples unto them, and said, It is not reason that we should leave the word of God, and serve tables.

3 Wherefore, brethren, look ye out among you seven men of honest report, full of the Holy Ghost and wisdom, whom we may appoint over this business.

4 But we will give ourselves continually to prayer, and to the ministry of the word.

5 And the saying pleased the whole multitude: and they chose Stephen, a man full of faith and of the Holy Ghost, and Philip, and Prochorus, and Nicanor, and Timon, and Parmenas, and Nicolas a proselyte of Antioch:

6 Whom they set before the apostles: and when they had prayed, they laid their hands on them.

7 And the word of God increased; and the number of the

Notes:

disciples multiplied in Jerusalem greatly; and a great company of the priests were obedient to the faith.

8 And Stephen, full of faith and power, did great wonders and miracles among the people.

9 Then there arose certain of the synagogue, which is called the synagogue of the Libertines, and Cyrenians, and Alexandrians, and of them of Cilicia and of Asia, disputing with Stephen.

10 And they were not able to resist the wisdom and the spirit by which he spake.

6:11: The men lied in order to have Stephen arrested.

11 Then they suborned men, which said, We have heard him speak blasphemous words against Moses, and against God.

12 And they stirred up the people, and the elders, and the scribes, and came upon him, and caught him, and brought him to the council,

6:13: More people lied about Stephen.

13 And set up false witnesses, which said, This man ceaseth not to speak blasphemous words against this holy place, and the law:

14 For we have heard him say, that this Jesus of Nazareth shall destroy this place, and shall change the customs which Moses delivered us.

15 And all that sat in the council, looking stedfastly on him, saw

his face as it had been the face of an angel.

Notes:

Acts Chapter 7

1 Then said the high priest, Are these things so?

2 And he said, Men, brethren, and fathers, hearken; The God of glory appeared unto our father Abraham, when he was in Mesopotamia, before he dwelt in Charran,

3 And said unto him, Get thee out of thy country, and from thy kindred, and come into the land which I shall shew thee.

4 Then came he out of the land of the Chaldaeans, and dwelt in Charran: and from thence, when his father was dead, he removed him into this land, wherein ye now dwell.

5 And he gave him none inheritance in it, no, not so much as to set his foot on: yet he promised that he would give it to him for a possession, and to his seed after him, when as yet he had no child.

6 And God spake on this wise, That his seed should sojourn in a strange land; and that they should bring them into bondage, and entreat them evil four hundred years.

Notes:

7 And the nation to whom they shall be in bondage will I judge, said God: and after that shall they come forth, and serve me in this place.

8 And he gave him the covenant of circumcision: and so Abraham begat Isaac, and circumcised him the eighth day; and Isaac begat Jacob; and Jacob begat the twelve patriarchs.

9 And the patriarchs, moved with envy, sold Joseph into Egypt: but God was with him,

10 And delivered him out of all his afflictions, and gave him favour and wisdom in the sight of Pharaoh king of Egypt; and he made him governor over Egypt and all his house.

11 Now there came a dearth over all the land of Egypt and Chanaan, and great affliction: and our fathers found no sustenance.

12 But when Jacob heard that there was corn in Egypt, he sent out our fathers first.

13 And at the second time Joseph was made known to his brethren; and Joseph's kindred was made known unto Pharaoh.

14 Then sent Joseph, and called his father Jacob to him, and all his kindred, threescore and fifteen souls.

15 So Jacob went down into Egypt, and died, he, and our fathers,

16 And were carried over into Sychem, and laid in the sepulchre that Abraham bought for a sum of money of the sons of Emmor the father of Sychem.

17 But when the time of the promise drew nigh, which God had sworn to Abraham, the people grew and multiplied in Egypt,

18 Till another king arose, which knew not Joseph.

19 The same dealt subtilly with our kindred, and evil entreated our fathers, so that they cast out their young children, to the end they might not live.

20 In which time Moses was born, and was exceeding fair, and nourished up in his father's house three months:

21 And when he was cast out, Pharaoh's daughter took him up, and nourished him for her own son.

22 And Moses was learned in all the wisdom of the Egyptians, and was mighty in words and in deeds.

23 And when he was full forty years old, it came into his heart to visit his brethren the children of Israel.

Notes:

24 And seeing one of them suffer wrong, he defended him, and avenged him that was oppressed, and smote the Egyptian:

25 For he supposed his brethren would have understood how that God by his hand would deliver them: but they understood not.

26 And the next day he shewed himself unto them as they strove, and would have set them at one again, saying, Sirs, ye are brethren; why do ye wrong one to another?

27 But he that did his neighbour wrong thrust him away, saying, Who made thee a ruler and a judge over us?

28 Wilt thou kill me, as thou diddest the Egyptian yesterday?

29 Then fled Moses at this saying, and was a stranger in the land of Madian, where he begat two sons.

30 And when forty years were expired, there appeared to him in the wilderness of mount Sina an angel of the Lord in a flame of fire in a bush.

31 When Moses saw it, he wondered at the sight: and as he drew near to behold it, the voice of the Lord came unto him,

32 Saying, I am the God of thy fathers, the God of Abrham, and

Notes:

the God of Isaac, and the God of Jacob. Then Moses trembled, and durst not behold.

33 Then said the Lord to him, Put off thy shoes from thy feet: for the place where thou standest is holy ground.

34 I have seen, I have seen the affliction of my people which is in Egypt, and I have heard their groaning, and am come down to deliver them. And now come, I will send thee into Egypt.

35 This Moses whom they refused, saying, Who made thee a ruler and a judge? the same did God send to be a ruler and a deliverer by the hand of the angel which appeared to him in the bush.

36 He brought them out, after that he had shewed wonders and signs in the land of Egypt, and in the Red sea, and in the wilderness forty years.

37 This is that Moses, which said unto the children of Israel, A prophet shall the Lord your God raise up unto you of your brethren, like unto me; him shall ye hear.

38 This is he, that was in the church in the wilderness with the angel which spake to him in the mount Sina, and with our fathers:

who received the lively oracles to
give unto us:

39 To whom our fathers would
not obey, but thrust him from them,
and in their hearts turned back
again into Egypt,

40 Saying unto Aaron, Make us
gods to go before us: for as for this
Moses, which brought us out of the
land of Egypt, we wot not what is
become of him.

41 And they made a calf in those
days, and offered sacrifice unto the
idol, and rejoiced in the works of
their own hands.

42 Then God turned, and gave
them up to worship the host of
heaven; as it is written in the book
of the prophets, O ye house of
Israel, have ye offered to me slain
beasts and sacrifices by the space of
forty years in the wilderness?

43 Yea, ye took up the tabernacle of Moloch, and the star of your
god Remphan, figures which ye
made to worship them: and I will
carry you away beyond Babylon.

44 Our fathers had the tabernacle of witness in the wilderness, as
he had appointed, speaking unto
Moses, that he should make it
according to the fashion that he had
seen.

45 Which also our fathers that came after brought in with Jesus into the possession of the Gentiles, whom God drave out before the face of our fathers, unto the days of David;

46 Who found favour before God, and desired to find a tabernacle for the God of Jacob.

47 But Solomon built him an house.

48 Howbeit the most High dwelleth not in temples made with hands; as saith the prophet,

49 Heaven is my throne, and earth is my footstool: what house will ye build me? saith the Lord: or what is the place of my rest?

50 Hath not my hand made all these things?

51 Ye stiffnecked and uncircumcised in heart and ears, ye do always resist the Holy Ghost: as your fathers did, so do ye.

52 Which of the prophets have not your fathers persecuted? and they have slain them which shewed before of the coming of the Just One; of whom ye have been now the betrayers and murderers:

53 Who have received the law by the disposition of angels, and have not kept it.

Notes:

7:53: The message that Stephen "preached" (see verses 2-53) detailed how the Israelites shunned the prophets and their messages from the time of Abraham unto the time of Jesus.

Notes:

54 When they heard these things, they were cut to the heart, and they gnashed on him with their teeth.

55 But he, being full of the Holy Ghost, looked up stedfastly into heaven, and saw the glory of God, and Jesus standing on the right hand of God,

56 And said, Behold, I see the heavens opened, and the Son of man standing on the right hand of God.

57 Then they cried out with a loud voice, and stopped their ears, and ran upon him with one accord,

58 And cast him out of the city, and stoned him: and the witnesses laid down their clothes at a young man's feet, whose name was Saul.

59 And they stoned Stephen, calling upon God, and saying, Lord Jesus, receive my spirit.

60 And he kneeled down, and cried with a loud voice, Lord, lay not this sin to their charge. And when he had said this, he fell asleep.

Acts Chapter 8

1 And Saul was consenting unto his death. And at that time there was a great persecution against the church which was at Jerusalem;

7:58: This is the first mention of Saul, who later became known as Paul, the Apostle who penned most of the New Testament epistles.

and they were all scattered abroad throughout the regions of Judaea and Samaria, except the apostles.

2 And devout men carried Stephen to his burial, and made great lamentation over him.

3 As for Saul, he made havock of the church, entering into every house, and haling men and women committed them to prison.

4 Therefore they that were scattered abroad went every where preaching the word.

5 Then Philip went down to the city of Samaria, and preached Christ unto them.

6 And the people with one accord gave heed unto those things which Philip spake, hearing and seeing the miracles which he did.

7 For unclean spirits, crying with loud voice, came out of many that were possessed with them: and many taken with palsies, and that were lame, were healed.

8 And there was great joy in that city.

9 But there was a certain man, called Simon, which beforetime in the same city used sorcery, and bewitched the people of Samaria, giving out that himself was some great one:

Notes:

8:3: Notice Saul (later known as the Apostle Paul), at first persecuted the Christians as a devout Jew. He believed they were against God and that their preaching was heresies.

8:4: This is when the message of Christ spread from Jerusalem to other parts of the world, as Christ instructed In Acts 1:8. It took persecution of the Jerusalem church to move the message into other parts of the world.

Notes:

8:12: Notice they were baptized. This was commanded in Acts 2:38 and they were following the instructions. Today, however, there are many false teachers that say baptism is not necessary to "be saved." What says the Word of God? (See Mark 16:16.)

8:16: Many today think that a person automatically receives the Holy Ghost at the time of being baptized. This passage disproves that, showing that receiving the Holy Ghost is a distinct experience, separate from baptism. Also, note that they were baptized in the "name of the Lord Jesus", not in the "name of the Father, and of the Son and of the Holy Ghost." They obeyed Acts 2:38.

10 To whom they all gave heed, from the least to the greatest, saying, This man is the great power of God.

11 And to him they had regard, because that of long time he had bewitched them with sorceries.

12 But when they believed Philip preaching the things concerning the kingdom of God, and the name of Jesus Christ, they were baptized, both men and women.

13 Then Simon himself believed also: and when he was baptized, he continued with Philip, and wondered, beholding the miracles and signs which were done.

14 Now when the apostles which were at Jerusalem heard that Samaria had received the word of God, they sent unto them Peter and John:

15 Who, when they were come down, prayed for them, that they might receive the Holy Ghost:

16 (For as yet he was fallen upon none of them: only they were baptized in the name of the Lord Jesus.)

17 Then laid they their hands on them, and they received the Holy Ghost.

18 And when Simon saw that through laying on of the apostles' hands the Holy Ghost was given, he offered them money,

19 Saying, Give me also this power, that on whomsoever I lay hands, he may receive the Holy Ghost.

20 But Peter said unto him, Thy money perish with thee, because thou hast thought that the gift of God may be purchased with money.

21 Thou hast neither part nor lot in this matter: for thy heart is not right in the sight of God.

22 Repent therefore of this thy wickedness, and pray God, if perhaps the thought of thine heart may be forgiven thee.

23 For I perceive that thou art in the gall of bitterness, and in the bond of iniquity.

24 Then answered Simon, and said, Pray ye to the Lord for me, that none of these things which ye have spoken come upon me.

25 And they, when they had testified and preached the word of the Lord, returned to Jerusalem, and

Notes:

8:19: The scripture does not say what Simon saw, only that they received the Holy Ghost and that Simon saw it. Based on other scriptures—to be discussed later—it is evident that Simon saw them speak with other tongues. This is how he knew that they received the Holy Ghost. Such was the evidence in that time, and it is the evidence today.

Notes:

preached the gospel in many villages of the Samaritans.

26 And the angel of the Lord spake unto Philip, saying, Arise, and go toward the south unto the way that goeth down from Jerusalem unto Gaza, which is desert.

27 And he arose and went: and, behold, a man of Ethiopia, an eunuch of great authority under Candace queen of the Ethiopians, who had the charge of all her treasure, and had come to Jerusalem for to worship,

28 Was returning, and sitting in his chariot read Esaias the prophet.

29 Then the Spirit said unto Philip, Go near, and join thyself to this chariot.

30 And Philip ran thither to him, and heard him read the prophet Esaias, and said, Understandest thou what thou readest?

31 And he said, How can I, except some man should guide me? And he desired Philip that he would come up and sit with him.

32 The place of the scripture which he read was this, He was led as a sheep to the slaughter; and like a lamb dumb before his shearer, so opened he not his mouth:

33 In his humiliation his judgment was taken away: and who shall declare his generation? for his life is taken from the earth.

34 And the eunuch answered Philip, and said, I pray thee, of whom speaketh the prophet this? of himself, or of some other man?

35 Then Philip opened his mouth, and began at the same scripture, and preached unto him Jesus.

36 And as they went on their way, they came unto a certain water: and the eunuch said, See, here is water; what doth hinder me to be baptized?

37 And Philip said, If thou believest with all thine heart, thou mayest. And he answered and said, I believe that Jesus Christ is the Son of God.

38 And he commanded the chariot to stand still: and they went down both into the water, both Philip and the eunuch; and he baptized him.

39 And when they were come up out of the water, the Spirit of the Lord caught away Philip, that the eunuch saw him no more: and he went on his way rejoicing.

40 But Philip was found at

Notes:

8:38: This is evidence that baptism is to be done by complete immersion. In the desert, where water is scarce, the scripture says that, "they both went down into the water." The "sprinkling" found in many churches today is different from immersion that is taught in the Bible. We need to be fully immersed to be baptized.

Notes:

Azotus: and passing through he preached in all the cities, till he came to Caesarea.

Acts Chapter 9

1 And Saul, yet breathing out threatenings and slaughter against the disciples of the Lord, went unto the high priest,

2 And desired of him letters to Damascus to the synagogues, that if he found any of this way, whether they were men or women, he might bring them bound unto Jerusalem.

3 And as he journeyed, he came near Damascus: and suddenly there shined round about him a light from heaven:

4 And he fell to the earth, and heard a voice saying unto him, Saul, Saul, why persecutest thou me?

5 And he said, Who art thou, Lord? And the Lord said, I am Jesus whom thou persecutest: it is hard for thee to kick against the pricks.

6 And he trembling and astonished said, Lord, what wilt thou have me to do? And the Lord said unto him, Arise, and go into the city, and it shall be told thee what thou must do.

7 And the men which journeyed with him stood speechless, hearing

9:5: It was here that Saul (later to be known as Paul) received the revelation about Jesus. Remember, Saul was persecuting the Christians and did not believe that Jesus was the Messiah. However, he clearly realized that the Lord God Himself was speaking to him here. When he asked God "who art thou" the Lord answered and said, "I am Jesus"—a great revelation of truth.

Notes:

a voice, but seeing no man.

8   And Saul arose from the earth; and when his eyes were opened, he saw no man: but they led him by the hand, and brought him into Damascus.

9   And he was three days without sight, and neither did eat nor drink.

10   And there was a certain disciple at Damascus, named Ananias; and to him said the Lord in a vision, Ananias. And he said, Behold, I am here, Lord.

11   And the Lord said unto him, Arise, and go into the street which is called Straight, and inquire in the house of Judas for one called Saul, of Tarsus: for, behold, he prayeth,

12   And hath seen in a vision a man named Ananias coming in, and putting his hand on him, that he might receive his sight.

13   Then Ananias answered, Lord, I have heard by many of this man, how much evil he hath done to thy saints at Jerusalem:

14   And here he hath authority from the chief priests to bind all that call on thy name.

15   But the Lord said unto him, Go thy way: for he is a chosen vessel unto me, to bear my name

Notes:

9:16: The path for the rest of Saul's life was set at this point, by God. He would become the most prolific writer of the New Testament, all words inspired by God Himself.

before the Gentiles, and kings, and the children of Israel:

16 For I will shew him how great things he must suffer for my name's sake.

17 And Ananias went his way, and entered into the house; and putting his hands on him said, Brother Saul, the Lord, even Jesus, that appeared unto thee in the way as thou camest, hath sent me, that thou mightest receive thy sight, and be filled with the Holy Ghost.

18 And immediately there fell from his eyes as it had been scales: and he received sight forthwith, and arose, and was baptized.

19 And when he had received meat, he was strengthened. Then was Saul certain days with the disciples which were at Damascus.

20 And straightway he preached Christ in the synagogues, that he is the Son of God.

21 But all that heard him were amazed, and said; Is not this he that destroyed them which called on this name in Jerusalem, and came hither for that intent, that he might bring them bound unto the chief priests?

22 But Saul increased the more in strength, and confounded the

Jews which dwelt at Damascus, proving that this is very Christ.

23 And after that many days were fulfilled, the Jews took counsel to kill him:

24 But their laying await was known of Saul. And they watched the gates day and night to kill him.

25 Then the disciples took him by night, and let him down by the wall in a basket.

26 And when Saul was come to Jerusalem, he assayed to join himself to the disciples: but they were all afraid of him, and believed not that he was a disciple.

27 But Barnabas took him, and brought him to the apostles, and declared unto them how he had seen the Lord in the way, and that he had spoken to him, and how he had preached boldly at Damascus in the name of Jesus.

28 And he was with them coming in and going out at Jerusalem.

29 And he spake boldly in the name of the Lord Jesus, and disputed against the Grecians: but they went about to slay him.

30 Which when the brethren knew, they brought him down to Caesarea, and sent him forth to Tarsus.

Notes:

9:25: This was the first escape from death that Saul (later to be known as Paul) experienced. Many more were to come as he preached the gospel.

Notes:

31 Then had the churches rest throughout all Judaea and Galilee and Samaria, and were edified; and walking in the fear of the Lord, and in the comfort of the Holy Ghost, were multiplied.

32 And it came to pass, as Peter passed throughout all quarters, he came down also to the saints which dwelt at Lydda.

33 And there he found a certain man named Aeneas, which had kept his bed eight years, and was sick of the palsy.

9:34: Another miracle of the Lord using Peter—healing of the palsy.

34 And Peter said unto him, Aeneas, Jesus Christ maketh thee whole: arise, and make thy bed. And he arose immediately.

35 And all that dwelt at Lydda and Saron saw him, and turned to the Lord.

36 Now there was at Joppa a certain disciple named Tabitha, which by interpretation is called Dorcas: this woman was full of good works and almsdeeds which she did.

37 And it came to pass in those days, that she was sick, and died: whom when they had washed, they laid her in an upper chamber.

38 And forasmuch as Lydda was nigh to Joppa, and the disciples had heard that Peter was there, they sent unto him two men, desiring him that he would not delay to come to them.

39 Then Peter arose and went with them. When he was come, they brought him into the upper chamber: and all the widows stood by him weeping, and shewing the coats and garments which Dorcas made, while she was with them.

40 But Peter put them all forth, and kneeled down, and prayed; and turning him to the body said, Tabitha, arise. And she opened her eyes: and when she saw Peter, she sat up.

41 And he gave her his hand, and lifted her up, and when he had called the saints and widows, presented her alive.

42 And it was known throughout all Joppa; and many believed in the Lord.

43 And it came to pass, that he tarried many days in Joppa with one Simon a tanner.

Acts Chapter 10

1 There was a certain man in Caesarea called Cornelius, a centurion of the band called the Italian band,

Notes:

9:41: Dorcas was raised from the dead by God through Peter.

Notes:

10:2: Notice how "good" this man was; he was spiritual, he feared God, he gave money to the poor and prayed always. But even though he was devout, he still had to obey Acts 2:38. This man might be compared to the devoted "Christians" of today who do all the "right" things. But are they really saved? Have they actually done the things instructed by God through His Apostles? Have they followed the plan of salvation found in Acts 2:38?

10:6: This man's prayers were a "memorial before God," yet he needed more and God sent Peter to tell him what he needed to do [to be saved].

2 A devout man, and one that feared God with all his house, which gave much alms to the people, and prayed to God alway.

3 He saw in a vision evidently about the ninth hour of the day an angel of God coming in to him, and saying unto him, Cornelius.

4 And when he looked on him, he was afraid, and said, What is it, Lord? And he said unto him, Thy prayers and thine alms are come up for a memorial before God.

5 And now send men to Joppa, and call for one Simon, whose surname is Peter:

6 He lodgeth with one Simon a tanner, whose house is by the sea side: he shall tell thee what thou oughtest to do.

7 And when the angel which spake unto Cornelius was departed, he called two of his household servants, and a devout soldier of them that waited on him continually;

8 And when he had declared all these things unto them, he sent them to Joppa.

9 On the morrow, as they

went on their journey, and drew nigh unto the city, Peter went up upon the housetop to pray about the sixth hour:

10 And he became very hungry, and would have eaten: but while they made ready, he fell into a trance,

11 And saw heaven opened, and a certain vessel descending unto him, as it had been a great sheet knit at the four corners, and let down to the earth:

12 Wherein were all manner of fourfooted beasts of the earth, and wild beasts, and creeping things, and fowls of the air.

13 And there came a voice to him, Rise, Peter; kill, and eat.

14 But Peter said, Not so, Lord; for I have never eaten any thing that is common or unclean.

15 And the voice spake unto him again the second time, What God hath cleansed, that call not thou common.

16 This was done thrice: and the vessel was received up again into heaven.

17 Now while Peter doubted in himself what this vision which he had seen should mean, behold, the men which were sent from

Cornelius had made inquiry for Simon's house, and stood before the gate,

18 And called, and asked whether Simon, which was surnamed Peter, were lodged there.

19 While Peter thought on the vision, the Spirit said unto him, Behold, three men seek thee.

20 Arise therefore, and get thee down, and go with them, doubting nothing: for I have sent them.

21 Then Peter went down to the men which were sent unto him from Cornelius; and said, Behold, I am he whom ye seek: what is the cause wherefore ye are come?

22 And they said, Cornelius the centurion, a just man, and one that feareth God, and of good report among all the nation of the Jews, was warned from God by an holy angel to send for thee into his house, and to hear words of thee.

23 Then called he them in, and lodged them. And on the morrow Peter went away with them, and certain brethren from Joppa accompanied him.

24 And the morrow after they entered into Caesarea. And Cornelius waited for them, and had called together his kinsmen and

Notes:

near friends.

25 And as Peter was coming in, Cornelius met him, and fell down at his feet, and worshipped him.

26 But Peter took him up, saying, Stand up; I myself also am a man.

10:26: No mere man should be worshipped, nor should any man ever allow men to kiss their hands or rings in worship.

27 And as he talked with him, he went in, and found many that were come together.

28 And he said unto them, Ye know how that it is an unlawful thing for a man that is a Jew to keep company, or come unto one of another nation; but God hath shewed me that I should not call any man common or unclean.

29 Therefore came I unto you without gainsaying, as soon as I was sent for: I ask therefore for what intent ye have sent for me?

30 And Cornelius said, Four days ago I was fasting until this hour; and at the ninth hour I prayed in my house, and, behold, a man stood before me in bright clothing,

31 And said, Cornelius, thy prayer is heard, and thine alms are had in remembrance in the sight of God.

32 Send therefore to Joppa, and call hither Simon, whose surname

Notes:

10:35: *"God is no respecter of persons."* God can accept anyone, just as the scripture says. Yet the believer must act upon faith by doing the things that we are commanded to do to "be saved."

is Peter; he is lodged in the house of one Simon a tanner by the sea side: who, when he cometh, shall speak unto thee.

33 Immediately therefore I sent to thee; and thou hast well done that thou art come. Now therefore are we all here present before God, to hear all things that are commanded thee of God.

34 Then Peter opened his mouth, and said, Of a truth I perceive that God is no respecter of persons:

35 But in every nation he that feareth him, and worketh righteousness, is accepted with him.

36 The word which God sent unto the children of Israel, preaching peace by Jesus Christ: (he is Lord of all:)

37 That word, I say, ye know, which was published throughout all Judaea, and began from Galilee, after the baptism which John preached;

38 How God anointed Jesus of Nazareth with the Holy Ghost and with power: who went about doing good, and healing all that were oppressed of the devil; for God was with him.

39 And we are witnesses of all

Notes:

things which he did both in the land of the Jews, and in Jerusalem; whom they slew and hanged on a tree:

40 Him God raised up the third day, and shewed him openly;

41 Not to all the people, but unto witnesses chosen before of God, even to us, who did eat and drink with him after he rose from the dead.

42 And he commanded us to preach unto the people, and to testify that it is he which was ordained of God to be the Judge of quick and dead.

43 To him give all the prophets witness, that through his name whosoever believeth in him shall receive remission of sins.

44 While Peter yet spake these words, the Holy Ghost fell on all them which heard the word.

45 And they of the circumcision which believed were astonished, as many as came with Peter, because that on the Gentiles also was poured out the gift of the Holy Ghost.

46 For they heard them speak with tongues, and magnify God. Then answered Peter,

47 Can any man forbid water, that these should not be baptized,

10:44-45: This was the first time that non-Jews (Gentiles) were filled with the Holy Ghost, proving that God's message is for everyone.

10:46: How did the Jews know the Gentiles had received the Spirit? "They heard them speak with tongues!"

73

Notes:

10:48: After receiving the Holy Ghost, they were baptized in the name of the Lord, which is Jesus (remember what Saul asked: "Who art thou Lord?" and the answer was Jesus—see Acts 9:5).

It should also be noted that there is no specific order to receiving the Holy Ghost and being baptized in Jesus name. After repentance, the New Birth (of both water and Spirit) must be experienced to fulfill the plan of salvation found in Acts 2:38.

which have received the Holy Ghost as well as we?

48 And he commanded them to be baptized in the name of the Lord. Then prayed they him to tarry certain days.

Acts Chapter 11

1 And the apostles and brethren that were in Judaea heard that the Gentiles had also received the word of God.

2 And when Peter was come up to Jerusalem, they that were of the circumcision contended with him,

3 Saying, Thou wentest in to men uncircumcised, and didst eat with them.

4 But Peter rehearsed the matter from the beginning, and expounded it by order unto them, saying,

5 I was in the city of Joppa praying: and in a trance I saw a vision, A certain vessel descend, as it had been a great sheet, let down from heaven by four corners; and it came even to me:

6 Upon the which when I had fastened mine eyes, I considered, and saw fourfooted beasts of the earth, and wild beasts, and creeping things, and fowls of the air.

7 And I heard a voice saying

Notes:

unto me, Arise, Peter; slay and eat.

8 But I said, Not so, Lord: for nothing common or unclean hath at any time entered into my mouth.

9 But the voice answered me again from heaven, What God hath cleansed, that call not thou common.

10 And this was done three times: and all were drawn up again into heaven.

11 And, behold, immediately there were three men already come unto the house where I was, sent from Caesarea unto me.

12 And the spirit bade me go with them, nothing doubting. Moreover these six brethren accompanied me, and we entered into the man's house:

13 And he shewed us how he had seen an angel in his house, which stood and said unto him, Send men to Joppa, and call for Simon, whose surname is Peter;

14 Who shall tell thee words, whereby thou and all thy house shall be saved.

15 And as I began to speak, the Holy Ghost fell on them, as on us at the beginning.

16 Then remembered I the word of the Lord, how that he said, John

11:15: The same Holy Ghost fell on the Gentiles as on the Jewish Apostles. How did they know? Because both spoke with other tongues. It is the outward, audible evidence of receiving the Holy Ghost.

indeed baptized with water; but ye shall be baptized with the Holy Ghost.

17 Forasmuch then as God gave them the like gift as he did unto us, who believed on the Lord Jesus Christ; what was I, that I could withstand God?

18 When they heard these things, they held their peace, and glorified God, saying, Then hath God also to the Gentiles granted repentance unto life.

19 Now they which were scattered abroad upon the persecution that arose about Stephen travelled as far as Phenice, and Cyprus, and Antioch, preaching the word to none but unto the Jews only.

20 And some of them were men of Cyprus and Cyrene, which, when they were come to Antioch, spake unto the Grecians, preaching the Lord Jesus.

21 And the hand of the Lord was with them: and a great number believed, and turned unto the Lord.

22 Then tidings of these things came unto the ears of the church which was in Jerusalem: and they sent forth Barnabas, that he should go as far as Antioch.

23 Who, when he came, and had

seen the grace of God, was glad,
and exhorted them all, that with
purpose of heart they would cleave
unto the Lord.

24 For he was a good man, and
full of the Holy Ghost and of faith:
and much people was added unto
the Lord.

25 Then departed Barnabas to
Tarsus, for to seek Saul:

26 And when he had found him,
he brought him unto Antioch. And
it came to pass, that a whole year
they assembled themselves with the
church, and taught much people.
And the disciples were called
Christians first in Antioch.

27 And in these days came
prophets from Jerusalem unto
Antioch.

28 And there stood up one of
them named Agabus, and signified
by the spirit that there should be
great dearth throughout all the
world: which came to pass in the
days of Claudius Caesar.

29 Then the disciples, every man
according to his ability, determined
to send relief unto the brethren
which dwelt in Judaea:

30 Which also they did, and sent
it to the elders by the hands of
Barnabas and Saul.

Notes:

Notes:

Acts Chapter 12

1 Now about that time Herod the king stretched forth his hands to vex certain of the church.

2 And he killed James the brother of John with the sword.

12:2: James was killed for preaching about Jesus, just as Stephen was.

3 And because he saw it pleased the Jews, he proceeded further to take Peter also. (Then were the days of unleavened bread.)

12:4: Peter was put in prison for preaching.

4 And when he had apprehended him, he put him in prison, and delivered him to four quaternions of soldiers to keep him; intending after Easter to bring him forth to the people.

5 Peter therefore was kept in prison: but prayer was made without ceasing of the church unto God for him.

6 And when Herod would have brought him forth, the same night Peter was sleeping between two soldiers, bound with two chains: and the keepers before the door kept the prison.

7 And, behold, the angel of the Lord came upon him, and a light shined in the prison: and he smote Peter on the side, and raised him up, saying, Arise up quickly. And his chains fell off from his hands.

8 And the angel said unto him,

Gird thyself, and bind on thy sandals. And so he did. And he saith unto him, Cast thy garment about thee, and follow me.

Notes:

9 And he went out, and followed him; and wist not that it was true which was done by the angel; but thought he saw a vision.

12:9: Peter was freed from prison by an angel.

10 When they were past the first and the second ward, they came unto the iron gate that leadeth unto the city; which opened to them of his own accord: and they went out, and passed on through one street; and forthwith the angel departed from him.

11 And when Peter was come to himself, he said, Now I know of a surety, that the Lord hath sent his angel, and hath delivered me out of the hand of Herod, and from all the expectation of the people of the Jews.

12 And when he had considered the thing, he came to the house of Mary the mother of John, whose surname was Mark; where many were gathered together praying.

13 And as Peter knocked at the door of the gate, a damsel came to hearken, named Rhoda.

14 And when she knew Peter's voice, she opened not the gate for

Notes:

gladness, but ran in, and told how Peter stood before the gate.

15 And they said unto her, Thou art mad. But she constantly affirmed that it was even so. Then said they, It is his angel.

16 But Peter continued knocking: and when they had opened the door, and saw him, they were astonished.

17 But he, beckoning unto them with the hand to hold their peace, declared unto them how the Lord had brought him out of the prison. And he said, Go shew these things unto James, and to the brethren. And he departed, and went into another place.

18 Now as soon as it was day, there was no small stir among the soldiers, what was become of Peter.

19 And when Herod had sought for him, and found him not, he examined the keepers, and commanded that they should be put to death. And he went down from Judaea to Caesarea, and there abode.

20 And Herod was highly displeased with them of Tyre and Sidon: but they came with one accord to him, and, having made Blastus the king's chamberlain their friend, desired peace; because their country was nourished by the king's country.

21 And upon a set day Herod, arrayed in royal apparel, sat upon his throne, and made an oration unto them.

22 And the people gave a shout, saying, It is the voice of a god, and not of a man.

23 And immediately the angel of the Lord smote him, because he gave not God the glory: and he was eaten of worms, and gave up the ghost.

24 But the word of God grew and multiplied.

25 And Barnabas and Saul returned from Jerusalem, when they had fulfilled their ministry, and took with them John, whose surname was Mark.

12:23: God smote Herod for accepting men's worship. How do you suppose God looks upon rock stars and movie stars today?

Acts Chapter 13

1 Now there were in the church that was at Antioch certain prophets and teachers; as Barnabas, and Simeon that was called Niger, and Lucius of Cyrene, and Manaen, which had been brought up with Herod the tetrarch, and Saul.

2 As they ministered to the Lord, and fasted, the Holy Ghost

Notes:

said, Separate me Barnabas and Saul for the work whereunto I have called them.

3 And when they had fasted and prayed, and laid their hands on them, they sent them away.

4 So they, being sent forth by the Holy Ghost, departed unto Seleucia; and from thence they sailed to Cyprus.

5 And when they were at Salamis, they preached the word of God in the synagogues of the Jews: and they had also John to their minister.

6 And when they had gone through the isle unto Paphos, they found a certain sorcerer, a false prophet, a Jew, whose name was Bar-jesus:

7 Which was with the deputy of the country, Sergius Paulus, a prudent man; who called for Barnabas and Saul, and desired to hear the word of God.

8 But Elymas the sorcerer (for so is his name by interpretation) withstood them, seeking to turn away the deputy from the faith.

13:9: This is the first reference to Saul as "Paul."

9 Then Saul, (who also is called Paul,) filled with the Holy Ghost, set his eyes on him,

10 And said, O full of all subtilty

and all mischief, thou child of the devil, thou enemy of all righteousness, wilt thou not cease to pervert the right ways of the Lord?

11 And now, behold, the hand of the Lord is upon thee, and thou shalt be blind, not seeing the sun for a season. And immediately there fell on him a mist and a darkness; and he went about seeking some to lead him by the hand.

12 Then the deputy, when he saw what was done, believed, being astonished at the doctrine of the Lord.

13 Now when Paul and his company loosed from Paphos, they came to Perga in Pamphylia: and John departing from them returned to Jerusalem.

14 But when they departed from Perga, they came to Antioch in Pisidia, and went into the synagogue on the sabbath day, and sat down.

15 And after the reading of the law and the prophets the rulers of the synagogue sent unto them, saying, Ye men and brethren, if ye have any word of exhortation for the people, say on.

16 Then Paul stood up, and beckoning with his hand said, Men

Notes:

13:11: A sorcerer with the power of Satan cannot withstand the superior power of a Spirit-filled saint of God.

Notes:

of Israel, and ye that fear God, give audience.

17 The God of this people of Israel chose our fathers, and exalted the people when they dwelt as strangers in the land of Egypt, and with an high arm brought he them out of it.

18 And about the time of forty years suffered he their manners in the wilderness.

19 And when he had destroyed seven nations in the land of Chanaan, he divided their land to them by lot.

20 And after that he gave unto them judges about the space of four hundred and fifty years, until Samuel the prophet.

21 And afterward they desired a king: and God gave unto them Saul the son of Cis, a man of the tribe of Benjamin, by the space of forty years.

22 And when he had removed him, he raised up unto them David to be their king; to whom also he gave testimony, and said, I have found David the son of Jesse, a man after mine own heart, which shall fulfil all my will.

23 Of this man's seed hath God according to his promise raised unto Israel a Saviour, Jesus:

24 When John had first preached before his coming the baptism of repentance to all the people of Israel.

25 And as John fulfilled his course, he said, Whom think ye that I am? I am not he. But, behold, there cometh one after me, whose shoes of his feet I am not worthy to loose.

26 Men and brethren, children of the stock of Abraham, and whosoever among you feareth God, to you is the word of this salvation sent.

27 For they that dwell at Jerusalem, and their rulers, because they knew him not, nor yet the voices of the prophets which are read every sabbath day, they have fulfilled them in condemning him.

28 And though they found no cause of death in him, yet desired they Pilate that he should be slain.

29 And when they had fulfilled all that was written of him, they took him down from the tree, and laid him in a sepulchre.

30 But God raised him from the dead:

31 And he was seen many days of them which came up with him from Galilee to Jerusalem, who are

Notes:

his witnesses unto the people.

32 And we declare unto you glad tidings, how that the promise which was made unto the fathers,

33 God hath fulfilled the same unto us their children, in that he hath raised up Jesus again; as it is also written in the second psalm, Thou art my Son, this day have I begotten thee.

34 And as concerning that he raised him up from the dead, now no more to return to corruption, he said on this wise, I will give you the sure mercies of David.

35 Wherefore he saith also in another psalm, Thou shalt not suffer thine Holy One to see corruption.

36 For David, after he had served his own generation by the will of God, fell on sleep, and was laid unto his fathers, and saw corruption:

37 But he, whom God raised again, saw no corruption.

38 Be it known unto you therefore, men and brethren, that through this man is preached unto you the forgiveness of sins:

39 And by him all that believe are justified from all things, from which ye could not be justified by the law of Moses.

40 Beware therefore, lest that come upon you, which is spoken of in the prophets;

41 Behold, ye despisers, and wonder, and perish: for I work a work in your days, a work which ye shall in no wise believe, though a man declare it unto you.

42 And when the Jews were gone out of the synagogue, the Gentiles besought that these words might be preached to them the next sabbath.

43 Now when the congregation was broken up, many of the Jews and religious proselytes followed Paul and Barnabas: who, speaking to them, persuaded them to continue in the grace of God.

44 And the next sabbath day came almost the whole city together to hear the word of God.

45 But when the Jews saw the multitudes, they were filled with envy, and spake against those things which were spoken by Paul, contradicting and blaspheming.

46 Then Paul and Barnabas waxed bold, and said, It was necessary that the word of God should first have been spoken to you: but seeing ye put it from you, and judge yourselves unworthy of ever-

Notes:

Notes:

lasting life, lo, we turn to the Gentiles.

47 For so hath the Lord commanded us, saying, I have set thee to be a light of the Gentiles, that thou shouldest be for salvation unto the ends of the earth.

48 And when the Gentiles heard this, they were glad, and glorified the word of the Lord: and as many as were ordained to eternal life believed.

49 And the word of the Lord was published throughout all the region.

50 But the Jews stirred up the devout and honourable women, and the chief men of the city, and raised persecution against Paul and Barnabas, and expelled them out of their coasts.

51 But they shook off the dust of their feet against them, and came unto Iconium.

52 And the disciples were filled with joy, and with the Holy Ghost.

Acts Chapter 14

1 And it came to pass in Iconium, that they went both together into the synagogue of the Jews, and so spake, that a great multitude both of the Jews and also of the Greeks believed.

2 But the unbelieving Jews stirred up the Gentiles, and made their minds evil affected against the brethren.

3 Long time therefore abode they speaking boldly in the Lord, which gave testimony unto the word of his grace, and granted signs and wonders to be done by their hands.

4 But the multitude of the city was divided: and part held with the Jews, and part with the apostles.

5 And when there was an assault made both of the Gentiles, and also of the Jews with their rulers, to use them despitefully, and to stone them,

6 They were ware of it, and fled unto Lystra and Derbe, cities of Lycaonia, and unto the region that lieth round about:

7 And there they preached the gospel.

8 And there sat a certain man at Lystra, impotent in his feet, being a cripple from his mother's womb, who never had walked:

9 The same heard Paul speak: who stedfastly beholding him, and perceiving that he had faith to be healed,

Notes:

Notes:

14:10: Through Paul, God healed a crippled man.

14:13-15: The men of the area witnessed the healing of the crippled man and set up to offer sacrifices to the Apostles. Their response was to stop them firmly and quickly.

10 Said with a loud voice, Stand upright on thy feet. And he leaped and walked.

11 And when the people saw what Paul had done, they lifted up their voices, saying in the speech of Lycaonia, The gods are come down to us in the likeness of men.

12 And they called Barnabas, Jupiter; and Paul, Mercurius, because he was the chief speaker.

13 Then the priest of Jupiter, which was before their city, brought oxen and garlands unto the gates, and would have done sacrifice with the people.

14 Which when the apostles, Barnabas and Paul, heard of, they rent their clothes, and ran in among the people, crying out,

15 And saying, Sirs, why do ye these things? We also are men of like passions with you, and preach unto you that ye should turn from these vanities unto the living God, which made heaven, and earth, and the sea, and all things that are therein:

16 Who in times past suffered all nations to walk in their own ways.

17 Nevertheless he left not himself without witness, in that he did good, and gave us rain from heaven, and fruitful seasons, filling our hearts with food and gladness.

18 And with these sayings scarce restrained they the people, that they had not done sacrifice unto them.

19 And there came thither certain Jews from Antioch and Iconium, who persuaded the people, and, having stoned Paul, drew him out of the city, supposing he had been dead.

Notes:

14:19: Paul was stoned and left for dead.

20 Howbeit, as the disciples stood round about him, he rose up, and came into the city: and the next day he departed with Barnabas to Derbe.

21 And when they had preached the gospel to that city, and had taught many, they returned again to Lystra, and to Iconium, and Antioch,

22 Confirming the souls of the disciples, and exhorting them to continue in the faith, and that we must through much tribulation enter into the kingdom of God.

23 And when they had ordained them elders in every church, and had prayed with fasting, they commended them to the Lord, on whom they believed.

24 And after they had passed throughout Pisidia, they came to Pamphylia.

25 And when they had preached the word in Perga, they went down into Attalia:

26 And thence sailed to Antioch, from whence they had been recommended to the grace of God for the work which they fulfilled.

27 And when they were come, and had gathered the church together, they rehearsed all that God had done with them, and how he had opened the door of faith unto the Gentiles.

28 And there they abode long time with the disciples.

Acts Chapter 15

1 And certain men which came down from Judaea taught the brethren, and said, Except ye be circumcised after the manner of Moses, ye cannot be saved.

2 When therefore Paul and Barnabas had no small dissension and disputation with them, they determined that Paul and Barnabas, and certain other of them, should go up to Jerusalem unto the apostles and elders about this question.

3 And being brought on their

Notes:

way by the church, they passed through Phenice and Samaria, declaring the conversion of the Gentiles: and they caused great joy unto all the brethren.

4 And when they were come to Jerusalem, they were received of the church, and of the apostles and elders, and they declared all things that God had done with them.

5 But there rose up certain of the sect of the Pharisees which believed, saying, That it was needful to circumcise them, and to command them to keep the law of Moses.

6 And the apostles and elders came together for to consider of this matter.

7 And when there had been much disputing, Peter rose up, and said unto them, Men and brethren, ye know how that a good while ago God made choice among us, that the Gentiles by my mouth should hear the word of the gospel, and believe.

8 And God, which knoweth the hearts, bare them witness, giving them the Holy Ghost, even as he did unto us;

9 And put no difference between us and them, purifying their hearts by faith.

10 Now therefore why tempt ye God, to put a yoke upon the neck of the disciples, which neither our fathers nor we were able to bear?

11 But we believe that through the grace of the Lord Jesus Christ we shall be saved, even as they.

12 Then all the multitude kept silence, and gave audience to Barnabas and Paul, declaring what miracles and wonders God had wrought among the Gentiles by them.

13 And after they had held their peace, James answered, saying, Men and brethren, hearken unto me:

14 Simeon hath declared how God at the first did visit the Gentiles, to take out of them a people for his name.

15 And to this agree the words of the prophets; as it is written,

16 After this I will return, and will build again the tabernacle of David, which is fallen down; and I will build again the ruins thereof, and I will set it up:

17 That the residue of men might seek after the Lord, and all the Gentiles, upon whom my name is called, saith the Lord, who doeth all these things.

18 Known unto God are all his

Notes:

works from the beginning of the world.

19 Wherefore my sentence is, that we trouble not them, which from among the Gentiles are turned to God:

20 But that we write unto them, that they abstain from pollutions of idols, and from fornication, and from things strangled, and from blood.

21 For Moses of old time hath in every city them that preach him, being read in the synagogues every sabbath day.

22 Then pleased it the apostles and elders, with the whole church, to send chosen men of their own company to Antioch with Paul and Barnabas; namely, Judas surnamed Barsabas, and Silas, chief men among the brethren:

23 And they wrote letters by them after this manner; The apostles and elders and brethren send greeting unto the brethren which are of the Gentiles in Antioch and Syria and Cilicia:

24 Forasmuch as we have heard, that certain which went out from us have troubled you with words, subverting your souls, saying, Ye must be circumcised, and keep the law:

Notes:

to whom we gave no such commandment:

25 It seemed good unto us, being assembled with one accord, to send chosen men unto you with our beloved Barnabas and Paul,

26 Men that have hazarded their lives for the name of our Lord Jesus Christ.

27 We have sent therefore Judas and Silas, who shall also tell you the same things by mouth.

28 For it seemed good to the Holy Ghost, and to us, to lay upon you no greater burden than these necessary things;

29 That ye abstain from meats offered to idols, and from blood, and from things strangled, and from fornication: from which if ye keep yourselves, ye shall do well. Fare ye well.

30 So when they were dismissed, they came to Antioch: and when they had gathered the multitude together, they delivered the epistle:

15:1-31: The physical act of circumcision was not required of the Gentiles.

31 Which when they had read, they rejoiced for the consolation.

32 And Judas and Silas, being prophets also themselves, exhorted the brethren with many words, and confirmed them.

33 And after they had tarried there a space, they were let go in peace from the brethren unto the apostles.

34 Notwithstanding it pleased Silas to abide there still.

35 Paul also and Barnabas continued in Antioch, teaching and preaching the word of the Lord, with many others also.

36 And some days after Paul said unto Barnabas, Let us go again and visit our brethren in every city where we have preached the word of the Lord, and see how they do.

37 And Barnabas determined to take with them John, whose surname was Mark.

38 But Paul thought not good to take him with them, who departed from them from Pamphylia, and went not with them to the work.

39 And the contention was so sharp between them, that they departed asunder one from the other: and so Barnabas took Mark, and sailed unto Cyprus;

40 And Paul chose Silas, and departed, being recommended by the brethren unto the grace of God.

41 And he went through Syria and Cilicia, confirming the churches.

Notes:

Notes:

Acts Chapter 16

1 Then came he to Derbe and Lystra: and, behold, a certain disciple was there, named Timotheus, the son of a certain woman, which was a Jewess, and believed; but his father was a Greek:

2 Which was well reported of by the brethren that were at Lystra and Iconium.

3 Him would Paul have to go forth with him; and took and circumcised him because of the Jews which were in those quarters: for they knew all that his father was a Greek.

4 And as they went through the cities, they delivered them the decrees for to keep, that were ordained of the apostles and elders which were at Jerusalem.

5 And so were the churches established in the faith, and increased in number daily.

6 Now when they had gone throughout Phrygia and the region of Galatia, and were forbidden of the Holy Ghost to preach the word in Asia,

7 After they were come to Mysia, they assayed to go into Bithynia: but the Spirit suffered them not.

16:5-6: This was the beginning of several churches in the region of Galatia, to which Paul later wrote an epistle to the Galatians.

16:6: The Holy Ghost guides and directs those who sincerely listen.

Notes:

8 And they passing by Mysia came down to Troas.

9 And a vision appeared to Paul in the night; There stood a man of Macedonia, and prayed him, saying, Come over into Macedonia, and help us.

10 And after he had seen the vision, immediately we endeavored to go into Macedonia, assuredly gathering that the Lord had called us for to preach the gospel unto them.

11 Therefore loosing from Troas, we came with a straight course to Samothracia, and the next day to Neapolis;

12 And from thence to Philippi, which is the chief city of that part of Macedonia, and a colony: and we were in that city abiding certain days.

16:12: It is here that the gospel of Christ was first preached in Philippi and a church was formed to which Paul later wrote his epistle to the Philippians.

13 And on the sabbath we went out of the city by a river side, where prayer was wont to be made; and we sat down, and spake unto the women which resorted thither.

14 And a certain woman named Lydia, a seller of purple, of the city of Thyatira, which worshipped God, heard us: whose heart the Lord opened, that she attended unto the things which were spoken of Paul.

Notes:

15 And when she was baptized, and her household, she besought us, saying, If ye have judged me to be faithful to the Lord, come into my house, and abide there. And she constrained us.

16 And it came to pass, as we went to prayer, a certain damsel possessed with a spirit of divination met us, which brought her masters much gain by soothsaying:

17 The same followed Paul and us, and cried, saying, These men are the servants of the most high God, which shew unto us the way of salvation.

16:18: Evil spirits are subject to the commands of a Spirit-filled saint of God.

18 And this did she many days. But Paul, being grieved, turned and said to the spirit, I command thee in the name of Jesus Christ to come out of her. And he came out the same hour.

19 And when her masters saw that the hope of their gains was gone, they caught Paul and Silas, and drew them into the marketplace unto the rulers,

20 And brought them to the magistrates, saying, These men, being Jews, do exceedingly trouble our city,

21 And teach customs, which are not lawful for us to receive, nei-

Notes:

ther to observe, being Romans.

22   And the multitude rose up together against them: and the magistrates rent off their clothes, and commanded to beat them.

23   And when they had laid many stripes upon them, they cast them into prison, charging the jailor to keep them safely:

24   Who, having received such a charge, thrust them into the inner prison, and made their feet fast in the stocks.

16:24: After being beaten, Paul and Silas were thrown into prison and their feet were placed in stocks.

25   And at midnight Paul and Silas prayed, and sang praises unto God: and the prisoners heard them.

26   And suddenly there was a great earthquake, so that the foundations of the prison were shaken: and immediately all the doors were opened, and every one's bands were loosed.

16:26: Even after beatings and while in stocks in prison, Paul and Silas sang and worshipped God. Whenever we are in troublesome situations, praise and worship to God frees the soul.

27   And the keeper of the prison awaking out of his sleep, and seeing the prison doors open, he drew out his sword, and would have killed himself, supposing that the prisoners had been fled.

28   But Paul cried with a loud voice, saying, Do thyself no harm: for we are all here.

29   Then he called for a light, and sprang in, and came trembling, and

Notes:

16:31: Some try to use this passage to nullify the importance of obeying Acts 2:38 because Paul and Silas answered very quickly, saying only to "believe on the Lord Jesus Christ." However, they later said more (see v. 32) in accordance with Acts 2:38, because the jailer and his whole house were baptized. Undoubtedly the jailer's threat of suicide prompted a quick answer, followed by more teaching.

fell down before Paul and Silas,

30 And brought them out, and said, Sirs, what must I do to be saved?

31 And they said, Believe on the Lord Jesus Christ, and thou shalt be saved, and thy house.

32 And they spake unto him the word of the Lord, and to all that were in his house.

33 And he took them the same hour of the night, and washed their stripes; and was baptized, he and all his, straightway.

34 And when he had brought them into his house, he set meat before them, and rejoiced, believing in God with all his house.

35 And when it was day, the magistrates sent the serjeants, saying, Let those men go.

36 And the keeper of the prison told this saying to Paul, The magistrates have sent to let you go: now therefore depart, and go in peace.

37 But Paul said unto them, They have beaten us openly uncondemned, being Romans, and have cast us into prison; and now do they thrust us out privily? nay verily; but let them come themselves and fetch us out.

38 And the serjeants told these

words unto the magistrates: and they feared, when they heard that they were Romans.

39 And they came and besought them, and brought them out, and desired them to depart out of the city.

40 And they went out of the prison, and entered into the house of Lydia and when they had seen the brethren, they comforted them, and departed.

Acts Chapter 17

1 Now when they had passed through Amphipolis and Apollonia, they came to Thessalonica, where was a synagogue of the Jews:

2 And Paul, as his manner was, went in unto them, and three sabbath days reasoned with them out of the scriptures,

3 Opening and alleging, that Christ must needs have suffered, and risen again from the dead; and that this Jesus, whom I preach unto you, is Christ.

4 And some of them believed, and consorted with Paul and Silas; and of the devout Greeks a great multitude, and of the chief women not a few.

Notes:

17:3: This is the first evidence of the founding of the church at Thessalonica to which Paul later wrote the epistles I and II Thessalonians.

Notes:

5 But the Jews which believed not, moved with envy, took unto them certain lewd fellows of the baser sort, and gathered a company, and set all the city on an uproar, and assaulted the house of Jason, and sought to bring them out to the people.

6 And when they found them not, they drew Jason and certain brethren unto the rulers of the city, crying, These that have turned the world upside down are come hither also;

7 Whom Jason hath received: and these all do contrary to the decrees of Caesar, saying that there is another king, one Jesus.

8 And they troubled the people and the rulers of the city, when they heard these things.

9 And when they had taken security of Jason, and of the other, they let them go.

10 And the brethren immediately sent away Paul and Silas by night unto Berea: who coming thither went into the synagogue of the Jews.

11 These were more noble than those in Thessalonica, in that they received the word with all readiness of mind, and searched the

17:10-11: We all ought to be like the "more noble" Bereans, who searched the scriptures daily to see if the preaching of the Apostles was biblical.

scriptures daily, whether those things were so.

12 Therefore many of them believed; also of honourable women which were Greeks, and of men, not a few.

13 But when the Jews of Thessalonica had knowledge that the word of God was preached of Paul at Berea, they came thither also, and stirred up the people.

14 And then immediately the brethren sent away Paul to go as it were to the sea: but Silas and Timotheus abode there still.

15 And they that conducted Paul brought him unto Athens: and receiving a commandment unto Silas and Timotheus for to come to him with all speed, they departed.

16 Now while Paul waited for them at Athens, his spirit was stirred in him, when he saw the city wholly given to idolatry.

17 Therefore disputed he in the synagogue with the Jews, and with the devout persons, and in the market daily with them that met with him.

18 Then certain philosophers of the Epicureans, and of the Stoicks, encountered him. And some said, What will this babbler say? other

Notes:

Notes:

some, He seemeth to be a setter forth of strange gods: because he preached unto them Jesus, and the resurrection.

19 And they took him, and brought him unto Areopagus, saying, May we know what this new doctrine, whereof thou speakest, is?

20 For thou bringest certain strange things to our ears: we would know therefore what these things mean.

21 (For all the Athenians and strangers which were there spent their time in nothing else, but either to tell, or to hear some new thing.)

22 Then Paul stood in the midst of Mars' hill, and said, Ye men of Athens, I perceive that in all things ye are too superstitious.

23 For as I passed by, and beheld your devotions, I found an altar with this inscription, TO THE UNKNOWN GOD. Whom therefore ye ignorantly worship, him declare I unto you.

24 God that made the world and all things therein, seeing that he is Lord of heaven and earth, dwelleth not in temples made with hands;

25 Neither is worshipped with men's hands, as though he needed any thing, seeing he giveth to all life, and breath, and all things;

26 And hath made of one blood all nations of men for to dwell on all the face of the earth, and hath determined the times before appointed, and the bounds of their habitation;

27 That they should seek the Lord, if haply they might feel after him, and find him, though he be not far from every one of us:

28 For in him we live, and move, and have our being; as certain also of your own poets have said, For we are also his offspring.

29 Forasmuch then as we are the offspring of God, we ought not to think that the Godhead is like unto gold, or silver, or stone, graven by art and man's device.

30 And the times of this ignorance God winked at; but now commandeth all men every where to repent:

31 Because he hath appointed a day, in the which he will judge the world in righteousness by that man whom he hath ordained; whereof he hath given assurance unto all men, in that he hath raised him from the dead.

32 And when they heard of the resurrection of the dead, some

Notes:

Notes:

mocked: and others said, We will hear thee again of this matter.

33 So Paul departed from among them.

34 Howbeit certain men clave unto him, and believed: among the which was Dionysius the Areopagite, and a woman named Damaris, and others with them.

Acts Chapter 18

18:1-2: This was the first time that Paul began to preach about Jesus in the city of Corinth, where a church was founded, to which later he wrote the epistles of I & II Corinthians.

1 After these things Paul departed from Athens, and came to Corinth;

2 And found a certain Jew named Aquila, born in Pontus, lately come from Italy, with his wife Priscilla; (because that Claudius had commanded all Jews to depart from Rome:) and came unto them.

3 And because he was of the same craft, he abode with them, and wrought: for by their occupation they were tentmakers.

4 And he reasoned in the synagogue every sabbath, and persuaded the Jews and the Greeks.

5 And when Silas and Timotheus were come from Macedonia, Paul was pressed in the spirit, and testified to the Jews that Jesus was Christ.

6 And when they opposed

themselves, and blasphemed, he shook his raiment, and said unto them, Your blood be upon your own heads; I am clean: from henceforth I will go unto the Gentiles.

7 And he departed thence, and entered into a certain man's house, named Justus, one that worshipped God, whose house joined hard to the synagogue.

8 And Crispus, the chief ruler of the synagogue, believed on the Lord with all his house; and many of the Corinthians hearing believed, and were baptized.

9 Then spake the Lord to Paul in the night by a vision, Be not afraid, but speak, and hold not thy peace:

10 For I am with thee, and no man shall set on thee to hurt thee: for I have much people in this city.

11 And he continued there a year and six months, teaching the word of God among them.

12 And when Gallio was the deputy of Achaia, the Jews made insurrection with one accord against Paul, and brought him to the judgment seat,

13 Saying, This fellow persuadeth men to worship God contrary to the law.

14 And when Paul was now

Notes:

Notes:

about to open his mouth, Gallio said unto the Jews, If it were a matter of wrong or wicked lewdness, O ye Jews, reason would that I should bear with you:

15 But if it be a question of words and names, and of your law, look ye to it; for I will be no judge of such matters.

16 And he drave them from the judgment seat.

17 Then all the Greeks took Sosthenes, the chief ruler of the synagogue, and beat him before the judgment seat. And Gallio cared for none of those things.

18 And Paul after this tarried there yet a good while, and then took his leave of the brethren, and sailed thence into Syria, and with him Priscilla and Aquila; having shorn his head in Cenchrea: for he had a vow.

18:19: This was the beginning of the church in the city of Ephesus, to which Paul later wrote his epistle to the Ephesians.

19 And he came to Ephesus, and left them there: but he himself entered into the synagogue, and reasoned with the Jews.

20 When they desired him to tarry longer time with them, he consented not;

21 But bade them farewell, saying, I must by all means keep this feast that cometh in Jerusalem: but I

will return again unto you, if God will. And he sailed from Ephesus.

22 And when he had landed at Caesarea, and gone up, and saluted the church, he went down to Antioch.

23 And after he had spent some time there, he departed, and went over all the country of Galatia and Phrygia in order, strengthening all the disciples.

24 And a certain Jew named Apollos, born at Alexandria, an eloquent man, and mighty in the scriptures, came to Ephesus.

25 This man was instructed in the way of the Lord; and being fervent in the spirit, he spake and taught diligently the things of the Lord, knowing only the baptism of John.

26 And he began to speak boldly in the synagogue: whom when Aquila and Priscilla had heard, they took him unto them, and expounded unto him the way of God more perfectly.

27 And when he was disposed to pass into Achaia, the brethren wrote, exhorting the disciples to receive him: who, when he was come, helped them much which had believed through grace:

Notes:

Notes:

19:2: *"Have ye received the Holy Ghost since ye believed?"* The question indicates that there is no automatic "tie" between believing and receiving the Spirit, just as there is no automatic accompaniment of the Spirit infilling upon water baptism. Believing and being water baptized are distinct from the Holy Ghost infilling. (See Acts 8, notes.)

19:4-5: Although these disciples of John the Baptist had already been baptized previously, they were rebaptized in Jesus name once the full truth was preached to them. Paul clearly taught (see I Corinthians 1:13) that we are to be baptized in the name of the one who was crucified for us—that name is Jesus. If you are not baptized in Jesus name, you need to be!

28 For he mightily convinced the Jews, and that publickly, shewing by the scriptures that Jesus was Christ.

Acts Chapter 19

1 And it came to pass, that, while Apollos was at Corinth, Paul having passed through the upper coasts came to Ephesus: and finding certain disciples,

2 He said unto them, Have ye received the Holy Ghost since ye believed? And they said unto him, We have not so much as heard whether there be any Holy Ghost.

3 And he said unto them, Unto what then were ye baptized? And they said, Unto John's baptism.

4 Then said Paul, John verily baptized with the baptism of repentance, saying unto the people, that they should believe on him which should come after him, that is, on Christ Jesus.

5 When they heard this, they were baptized in the name of the Lord Jesus.

6 And when Paul had laid

his hands upon them, the Holy Ghost came on them; and they spake with tongues, and prophesied.

7 And all the men were about twelve.

8 And he went into the synagogue, and spake boldly for the space of three months, disputing and persuading the things concerning the kingdom of God.

9 But when divers were hardened, and believed not, but spake evil of that way before the multitude, he departed from them, and separated the disciples, disputing daily in the school of one Tyrannus.

10 And this continued by the space of two years; so that all they which dwelt in Asia heard the word of the Lord Jesus, both Jews and Greeks.

11 And God wrought special miracles by the hands of Paul:

12 So that from his body were brought unto the sick handkerchiefs or aprons, and the diseases departed from them, and the evil spirits went out of them.

13 Then certain of the vagabond Jews, exorcists, took upon them to call over them which had evil spirits the name of the Lord Jesus, saying, We adjure you by Jesus whom

Notes:

19:6: How did they know the men received the Spirit baptism? Because the men spoke with tongues. How can you (or anyone else alive today) know that you have been filled with the Holy Ghost? By the very same evidence!

Notes:

Paul preacheth.

14 And there were seven sons of one Sceva, a Jew, and chief of the priests, which did so.

15 And the evil spirit answered and said, Jesus I know, and Paul I know; but who are ye?

16 And the man in whom the evil spirit was leaped on them, and overcame them, and prevailed against them, so that they fled out of that house naked and wounded.

17 And this was known to all the Jews and Greeks also dwelling at Ephesus; and fear fell on them all, and the name of the Lord Jesus was magnified.

18 And many that believed came, and confessed, and shewed their deeds.

19 Many of them also which used curious arts brought their books together, and burned them before all men: and they counted the price of them, and found it fifty thousand pieces of silver.

20 So mightily grew the word of God and prevailed.

21 After these things were ended, Paul purposed in the spirit, when he had passed through Macedonia and Achaia, to go to Jerusalem, saying, After I have been

Notes:

there, I must also see Rome.

22 So he sent into Macedonia two of them that ministered unto him, Timotheus and Erastus; but he himself stayed in Asia for a season.

23 And the same time there arose no small stir about that way.

24 For a certain man named Demetrius, a silversmith, which made silver shrines for Diana, brought no small gain unto the craftsmen;

25 Whom he called together with the workmen of like occupation, and said, Sirs, ye know that by this craft we have our wealth.

26 Moreover ye see and hear, that not alone at Ephesus, but almost throughout all Asia, this Paul hath persuaded and turned away much people, saying that they be no gods, which are made with hands:

27 So that not only this our craft is in danger to be set at nought; but also that the temple of the great goddess Diana should be despised, and her magnificence should be destroyed, whom all Asia and the world worshippeth.

28 And when they heard these sayings, they were full of wrath, and cried out, saying, Great is

Notes:

Diana of the Ephesians.

29 And the whole city was filled with confusion: and having caught Gaius and Aristarchus, men of Macedonia, Paul's companions in travel, they rushed with one accord into the theatre.

30 And when Paul would have entered in unto the people, the disciples suffered him not.

31 And certain of the chief of Asia, which were his friends, sent unto him, desiring him that he would not adventure himself into the theatre.

32 Some therefore cried one thing, and some another: for the assembly was confused; and the more part knew not wherefore they were come together.

33 And they drew Alexander out of the multitude, the Jews putting him forward. And Alexander beckoned with the hand, and would have made his defence unto the people.

34 But when they knew that he was a Jew, all with one voice about the space of two hours cried out, Great is Diana of the Ephesians.

35 And when the townclerk had appeased the people, he said, Ye men of Ephesus, what man is there that knoweth not how that the city of the Ephesians is a worshipper of the great goddess Diana, and of the image which fell down from Jupiter?

36 Seeing then that these things cannot be spoken against, ye ought to be quiet, and to do nothing rashly.

37 For ye have brought hither these men, which are neither robbers of churches, nor yet blasphemers of your goddess.

38 Wherefore if Demetrius, and the craftsmen which are with him, have a matter against any man, the law is open, and there are deputies: let them implead one another.

39 But if ye inquire any thing concerning other matters, it shall be determined in a lawful assembly.

40 For we are in danger to be called in question for this day's uproar, there being no cause whereby we may give an account of this concourse.

41 And when he had thus spoken, he dismissed the assembly.

Acts Chapter 20

1 And after the uproar was ceased, Paul called unto him the disciples, and embraced them, and departed for to go into Macedonia.

Notes:

Notes:

2 And when he had gone over those parts, and had given them much exhortation, he came into Greece,

3 And there abode three months. And when the Jews laid wait for him, as he was about to sail into Syria, he purposed to return through Macedonia.

4 And there accompanied him into Asia Sopater of Berea; and of the Thessalonians, Aristarchus and Secundus; and Gaius of Derbe, and Timotheus; and of Asia, Tychicus and Trophimus.

5 These going before tarried for us at Troas.

6 And we sailed away from Philippi after the days of unleavened bread, and came unto them to Troas in five days; where we abode seven days.

7 And upon the first day of the week, when the disciples came together to break bread, Paul preached unto them, ready to depart on the morrow; and continued his speech until midnight.

8 And there were many lights in the upper chamber, where they were gathered together.

9 And there sat in a window a certain young man named

Notes:

Eutychus, being fallen into a deep sleep: and as Paul was long preaching, he sunk down with sleep, and fell down from the third loft, and was taken up dead.

10 And Paul went down, and fell on him, and embracing him said, Trouble not yourselves; for his life is in him.

11 When he therefore was come up again, and had broken bread, and eaten, and talked a long while, even till break of day, so he departed.

12 And they brought the young man alive, and were not a little comforted.

13 And we went before to ship, and sailed unto Assos, there intending to take in Paul: for so had he appointed, minding himself to go afoot.

14 And when he met with us at Assos, we took him in, and came to Mitylene.

15 And we sailed thence, and came the next day over against Chios; and the next day we arrived at Samos, and tarried at Trogyllium; and the next day we came to Miletus.

16 For Paul had determined to sail by Ephesus, because he would not spend the time in Asia: for he hasted, if it were possible for him, to be at Jerusalem the day of Pentecost.

17 And from Miletus he sent to Ephesus, and called the elders of the church.

18 And when they were come to him, he said unto them, Ye know, from the first day that I came into Asia, after what manner I have been with you at all seasons,

19 Serving the Lord with all humility of mind, and with many tears, and temptations, which befell me by the lying in wait of the Jews:

20 And how I kept back nothing that was profitable unto you, but have shewed you, and have taught you publickly, and from house to house,

21 Testifying both to the Jews, and also to the Greeks, repentance toward God, and faith toward our Lord Jesus Christ.

22 And now, behold, I go bound in the spirit unto Jerusalem, not knowing the things that shall befall me there:

23 Save that the Holy Ghost witnesseth in every city, saying that bonds and afflictions abide me.

24 But none of these things

move me, neither count I my life dear unto myself, so that I might finish my course with joy, and the ministry, which I have received of the Lord Jesus, to testify the gospel of the grace of God.

25 And now, behold, I know that ye all, among whom I have gone preaching the kingdom of God, shall see my face no more.

26 Wherefore I take you to record this day, that I am pure from the blood of all men.

27 For I have not shunned to declare unto you all the counsel of God.

28 Take heed therefore unto yourselves, and to all the flock, over the which the Holy Ghost hath made you overseers, to feed the church of God, which he hath purchased with his own blood.

29 For I know this, that after my departing shall grievous wolves enter in among you, not sparing the flock.

30 Also of your own selves shall men arise, speaking perverse things, to draw away disciples after them.

31 Therefore watch, and remember, that by the space of three years I ceased not to warn every one night and day with tears.

Notes:

Notes:

32 And now, brethren, I commend you to God, and to the word of his grace, which is able to build you up, and to give you an inheritance among all them which are sanctified.

33 I have coveted no man's silver, or gold, or apparel.

34 Yea, ye yourselves know, that these hands have ministered unto my necessities, and to them that were with me.

35 I have shewed you all things, how that so labouring ye ought to support the weak, and to remember the words of the Lord Jesus, how he said, It is more blessed to give than to receive.

36 And when he had thus spoken, he kneeled down, and prayed with them all.

37 And they all wept sore, and fell on Paul's neck, and kissed him,

38 Sorrowing most of all for the words which he spake, that they should see his face no more. And they accompanied him unto the ship.

Acts Chapter 21

1 And it came to pass, that after we were gotten from them, and had launched, we came with a straight

Notes:

course unto Coos, and the day following unto Rhodes, and from
thence unto Patara:

2 And finding a ship sailing
over unto Phenicia, we went
aboard, and set forth.

3 Now when we had discovered
Cyprus, we left it on the left hand,
and sailed into Syria, and landed at
Tyre: for there the ship was to
unlade her burden.

4 And finding disciples, we tarried there seven days: who said to
Paul through the Spirit, that he
should not go up to Jerusalem.

5 And when we had accom-
plished those days, we departed
and went our way; and they all
brought us on our way, with wives
and children, till we were out of the
city: and we kneeled down on the
shore, and prayed.

6 And when we had taken our
leave one of another, we took ship;
and they returned home again.

7 And when we had finished
our course from Tyre, we came to
Ptolemais, and saluted the brethren,
and abode with them one day.

8 And the next day we that were
of Paul's company departed, and
came unto Caesarea: and we
entered into the house of Philip the

evangelist, which was one of the seven; and abode with him.

9 And the same man had four daughters, virgins, which did prophesy.

10 And as we tarried there many days, there came down from Judaea a certain prophet, named Agabus.

11 And when he was come unto us, he took Paul's girdle, and bound his own hands and feet, and said, Thus saith the Holy Ghost, So shall the Jews at Jerusalem bind the man that owneth this girdle, and shall deliver him into the hands of the Gentiles.

12 And when we heard these things, both we, and they of that place, besought him not to go up to Jerusalem.

13 Then Paul answered, What mean ye to weep and to break mine heart? for I am ready not to be bound only, but also to die at Jerusalem for the name of the Lord Jesus.

14 And when he would not be persuaded, we ceased, saying, The will of the Lord be done.

15 And after those days we took up our carriages, and went up to Jerusalem.

16 There went with us also certain of the disciples of Caesarea, and brought with them one Mnason of Cyprus, an old disciple, with whom we should lodge.

17 And when we were come to Jerusalem, the brethren received us gladly.

18 And the day following Paul went in with us unto James; and all the elders were present.

19 And when he had saluted them, he declared particularly what things God had wrought among the Gentiles by his ministry.

20 And when they heard it, they glorified the Lord, and said unto him, Thou seest, brother, how many thousands of Jews there are which believe; and they are all zealous of the law:

21 And they are informed of thee, that thou teachest all the Jews which are among the Gentiles to forsake Moses, saying that they ought not to circumcise their children, neither to walk after the customs.

22 What is it therefore? the multitude must needs come together: for they will hear that thou art come.

23 Do therefore this that we say

Notes:

to thee: We have four men which have a vow on them;

24 Them take, and purify thyself with them, and be at charges with them, that they may shave their heads: and all may know that those things, whereof they were informed concerning thee, are nothing; but that thou thyself also walkest orderly, and keepest the law.

25 As touching the Gentiles which believe, we have written and concluded that they observe no such thing, save only that they keep themselves from things offered to idols, and from blood, and from strangled, and from fornication.

26 Then Paul took the men, and the next day purifying himself with them entered into the temple, to signify the accomplishment of the days of purification, until that an offering should be offered for every one of them.

27 And when the seven days were almost ended, the Jews which were of Asia, when they saw him in the temple, stirred up all the people, and laid hands on him,

28 Crying out, Men of Israel, help: This is the man, that teacheth all men every where against the people, and the law, and this place:

and further brought Greeks also into the temple, and hath polluted this holy place.

29 (For they had seen before with him in the city Trophimus an Ephesian, whom they supposed that Paul had brought into the temple.)

30 And all the city was moved, and the people ran together: and they took Paul, and drew him out of the temple: and forthwith the doors were shut.

31 And as they went about to kill him, tidings came unto the chief captain of the band, that all Jerusalem was in an uproar.

32 Who immediately took soldiers and centurions, and ran down unto them: and when they saw the chief captain and the soldiers, they left beating of Paul.

33 Then the chief captain came near, and took him, and commanded him to be bound with two chains; and demanded who he was, and what he had done.

34 And some cried one thing, some another, among the multitude: and when he could not know the certainty for the tumult, he commanded him to be carried into the castle.

Notes:

35 And when he came upon the stairs, so it was, that he was borne of the soldiers for the violence of the people.

36 For the multitude of the people followed after, crying, Away with him.

37 And as Paul was to be led into the castle, he said unto the chief captain, May I speak unto thee? Who said, Canst thou speak Greek?

38 Art not thou that Egyptian, which before these days madest an uproar, and leddest out into the wilderness four thousand men that were murderers?

39 But Paul said, I am a man which am a Jew of Tarsus, a city in Cilicia, a citizen of no mean city: and, I beseech thee, suffer me to speak unto the people.

40 And when he had given him licence, Paul stood on the stairs, and beckoned with the hand unto the people. And when there was made a great silence, he spake unto them in the Hebrew tongue, saying,

Acts Chapter 22

1 Men, brethren, and fathers, hear ye my defence which I make now unto you.

Notes:

2 (And when they heard that he spake in the Hebrew tongue to them, they kept the more silence: and he saith,)

3 I am verily a man which am a Jew, born in Tarsus, a city in Cilicia, yet brought up in this city at the feet of Gamaliel, and taught according to the perfect manner of the law of the fathers, and was zealous toward God, as ye all are this day.

4 And I persecuted this way unto the death, binding and delivering into prisons both men and women.

5 As also the high priest doth bear me witness, and all the estate of the elders: from whom also I received letters unto the brethren, and went to Damascus, to bring them which were there bound unto Jerusalem, for to be punished.

6 And it came to pass, that, as I made my journey, and was come nigh unto Damascus about noon, suddenly there shone from heaven a great light round about me.

7 And I fell unto the ground, and heard a voice saying unto me, Saul, Saul, why persecutest thou me?

8 And I answered, Who art thou, Lord? And he said unto me, I am Jesus of Nazareth, whom thou persecutest.

9 And they that were with me saw indeed the light, and were afraid; but they heard not the voice of him that spake to me.

10 And I said, What shall I do, Lord? And the Lord said unto me, Arise, and go into Damascus; and there it shall be told thee of all things which are appointed for thee to do.

11 And when I could not see for the glory of that light, being led by the hand of them that were with me, I came into Damascus.

12 And one Ananias, a devout man according to the law, having a good report of all the Jews which dwelt there,

13 Came unto me, and stood, and said unto me, Brother Saul, receive thy sight. And the same hour I looked up upon him.

14 And he said, The God of our fathers hath chosen thee, that thou shouldest know his will, and see that Just One, and shouldest hear the voice of his mouth.

15 For thou shalt be his witness unto all men of what thou hast seen and heard.

16 And now why tarriest thou?

arise, and be baptized, and wash away thy sins, calling on the name of the Lord.

17 And it came to pass, that, when I was come again to Jerusalem, even while I prayed in the temple, I was in a trance;

18 And saw him saying unto me, Make haste, and get thee quickly out of Jerusalem: for they will not receive thy testimony concerning me.

19 And I said, Lord, they know that I imprisoned and beat in every synagogue them that believed on thee:

20 And when the blood of thy martyr Stephen was shed, I also was standing by, and consenting unto his death, and kept the raiment of them that slew him.

21 And he said unto me, Depart: for I will send thee far hence unto the Gentiles.

22 And they gave him audience unto this word, and then lifted up their voices, and said, Away with such a fellow from the earth: for it is not fit that he should live.

23 And as they cried out, and cast off their clothes, and threw dust into the air,

24 The chief captain command-

Notes:

ed him to be brought into the castle, and bade that he should be examined by scourging; that he might know wherefore they cried so against him.

25 And as they bound him with thongs, Paul said unto the centurion that stood by, Is it lawful for you to scourge a man that is a Roman, and uncondemned?

26 When the centurion heard that, he went and told the chief captain, saying, Take heed what thou doest: for this man is a Roman.

27 Then the chief captain came, and said unto him, Tell me, art thou a Roman? He said, Yea.

28 And the chief captain answered, With a great sum obtained I this freedom. And Paul said, But I was free born.

29 Then straightway they departed from him which should have examined him: and the chief captain also was afraid, after he knew that he was a Roman, and because he had bound him.

30 On the morrow, because he would have known the certainty wherefore he was accused of the Jews, he loosed him from his bands, and commanded the chief priests and all their council to appear, and

brought Paul down, and set him
before them.

Notes:

Acts Chapter 23

1 And Paul, earnestly beholding
the council, said, Men and brethren,
I have lived in all good conscience
before God until this day.

2 And the high priest Ananias
commanded them that stood by
him to smite him on the mouth.

3 Then said Paul unto him, God
shall smite thee, thou whited wall:
for sittest thou to judge me after the
law, and commandest me to be
smitten contrary to the law?

4 And they that stood by said,
Revilest thou God's high priest?

5 Then said Paul, I wist not,
brethren, that he was the high
priest: for it is written, Thou shalt
not speak evil of the ruler of thy
people.

6 But when Paul perceived that
the one part were Sadducees, and
the other Pharisees, he cried out in
the council, Men and brethren, I am
a Pharisee, the son of a Pharisee: of
the hope and resurrection of the
dead I am called in question.

7 And when he had so said,
there arose a dissension between
the Pharisees and the Sadducees:

Notes:

and the multitude was divided.

8 For the Sadducees say that there is no resurrection, neither angel, nor spirit: but the Pharisees confess both.

9 And there arose a great cry: and the scribes that were of the Pharisees' part arose, and strove, saying, We find no evil in this man: but if a spirit or an angel hath spoken to him, let us not fight against God.

10 And when there arose a great dissension, the chief captain, fearing lest Paul should have been pulled in pieces of them, commanded the soldiers to go down, and to take him by force from among them, and to bring him into the castle.

23:11: At Christ's instruction, Paul went to Rome, and through his preaching the church was formed there, to which Paul later wrote the epistle of Romans.

11 And the night following the Lord stood by him, and said, Be of good cheer, Paul: for as thou hast testified of me in Jerusalem, so must thou bear witness also at Rome.

12 And when it was day, certain of the Jews banded together, and bound themselves under a curse, saying that they would neither eat nor drink till they had killed Paul.

13 And they were more than forty which had made this conspiracy.

14 And they came to the chief

Notes:

priests and elders, and said, We have bound ourselves under a great curse, that we will eat nothing until we have slain Paul.

15 Now therefore ye with the council signify to the chief captain that he bring him down unto you to morrow, as though ye would inquire something more perfectly concerning him: and we, or ever he come near, are ready to kill him.

16 And when Paul's sister's son heard of their lying in wait, he went and entered into the castle, and told Paul.

17 Then Paul called one of the centurions unto him, and said, Bring this young man unto the chief captain: for he hath a certain thing to tell him

18 So he took him, and brought him to the chief captain, and said, Paul the prisoner called me unto him, and prayed me to bring this young man unto thee, who hath something to say unto thee.

19 Then the chief captain took him by the hand, and went with him aside privately, and asked him, What is that thou hast to tell me?

20 And he said, The Jews have agreed to desire thee that thou wouldest bring down Paul to mor-

Notes:

row into the council, as though they would inquire somewhat of him more perfectly.

21 But do not thou yield unto them: for there lie in wait for him of them more than forty men, which have bound themselves with an oath, that they will neither eat nor drink till they have killed him: and now are they ready, looking for a promise from thee.

22 So the chief captain then let the young man depart, and charged him, See thou tell no man that thou hast shewed these things to me.

23 And he called unto him two centurions, saying, Make ready two hundred soldiers to go to Caesarea, and horsemen threescore and ten, and spearmen two hundred, at the third hour of the night;

24 And provide them beasts, that they may set Paul on, and bring him safe unto Felix the governor.

25 And he wrote a letter after this manner:

26 Claudius Lysias unto the most excellent governor Felix sendeth greeting.

27 This man was taken of the Jews, and should have been killed of them: then came I with an army, and rescued him, having under-

Notes:

stood that he was a Roman.

28 And when I would have known the cause wherefore they accused him, I brought him forth into their council:

29 Whom I perceived to be accused of questions of their law, but to have nothing laid to his charge worthy of death or of bonds.

30 And when it was told me how that the Jews laid wait for the man, I sent straightway to thee, and gave commandment to his accusers also to say before thee what they had against him. Farewell.

31 Then the soldiers, as it was commanded them, took Paul, and brought him by night to Antipatris.

32 On the morrow they left the horsemen to go with him, and returned to the castle:

33 Who, when they came to Caesarea, and delivered the epistle to the governor, presented Paul also before him.

34 And when the governor had read the letter, he asked of what province he was. And when he understood that he was of Cilicia;

35 I will hear thee, said he, when thine accusers are also come. And he commanded him to be kept in Herod's judgment hall.

Acts Chapter 24

1 And after five days Ananias the high priest descended with the elders, and with a certain orator named Tertullus, who informed the governor against Paul.

2 And when he was called forth, Tertullus began to accuse him, saying, Seeing that by thee we enjoy great quietness, and that very worthy deeds are done unto this nation by thy providence,

3 We accept it always, and in all places, most noble Felix, with all thankfulness.

4 Notwithstanding, that I be not further tedious unto thee, I pray thee that thou wouldest hear us of thy clemency a few words.

5 For we have found this man a pestilent fellow, and a mover of sedition among all the Jews throughout the world, and a ringleader of the sect of the Nazarenes:

6 Who also hath gone about to profane the temple: whom we took, and would have judged according to our law.

7 But the chief captain Lysias came upon us, and with great violence took him away out of our hands,

8 Commanding his accusers to

Notes:

come unto thee: by examining of whom thyself mayest take knowledge of all these things, whereof we accuse him.

9 And the Jews also assented, saying that these things were so.

10 Then Paul, after that the governor had beckoned unto him to speak, answered, Forasmuch as I know that thou hast been of many years a judge unto this nation, I do the more cheerfully answer for myself:

11 Because that thou mayest understand, that there are yet but twelve days since I went up to Jerusalem for to worship.

12 And they neither found me in the temple disputing with any man, neither raising up the people, neither in the synagogues, nor in the city:

13 Neither can they prove the things whereof they now accuse me.

14 But this I confess unto thee, that after the way which they call heresy, so worship I the God of my fathers, believing all things which are written in the law and in the prophets:

15 And have hope toward God, which they themselves also allow, that there shall be a resurrection of

Notes:

the dead, both of the just and unjust.

16 And herein do I exercise myself, to have always a conscience void of offence toward God, and toward men.

17 Now after many years I came to bring alms to my nation, and offerings.

18 Whereupon certain Jews from Asia found me purified in the temple, neither with multitude, nor with tumult.

19 Who ought to have been here before thee, and object, if they had ought against me.

20 Or else let these same here say, if they have found any evil doing in me, while I stood before the council,

21 Except it be for this one voice, that I cried standing among them, Touching the resurrection of the dead I am called in question by you this day.

22 And when Felix heard these things, having more perfect knowledge of that way, he deferred them, and said, When Lysias the chief captain shall come down, I will know the uttermost of your matter.

23 And he commanded a centurion to keep Paul, and to let him

Notes:

have liberty, and that he should forbid none of his acquaintance to
minister or come unto him.

24 And after certain days, when
Felix came with his wife Drusilla,
which was a Jewess, he sent for
Paul, and heard him concerning the
faith in Christ.

25 And as he reasoned of righteousness, temperance, and judgment to come Felix trembled, and
answered, Go thy way for this time;
when I have a convenient season, I
will call for thee.

26 He hoped also that money
should have been given him of
Paul, that he might loose him:
wherefore he sent for him the often-
er, and communed with him.

27 But after two years Porcius
Festus came into Felix' room: and
Felix, willing to shew the Jews a
pleasure, left Paul bound.

Acts Chapter 25

1 Now when Festus was come
into the province, after three days
he ascended from Caesarea to
Jerusalem.

2 Then the high priest and the
chief of the Jews informed him
against Paul, and besought him,

3 And desired favour against

him, that he would send for him to
Jerusalem, laying wait in the way to
kill him.

4 But Festus answered, that Paul
should be kept at Caesarea, and
that he himself would depart short-
ly thither.

5 Let them therefore, said he,
which among you are able, go down
with me, and accuse this man, if
there be any wickedness in him.

6 And when he had tarried
among them more than ten days, he
went down unto Caesarea; and the
next day sitting on the judgment
seat commanded Paul to be
brought.

7 And when he was come, the
Jews which came down from
Jerusalem stood round about, and
laid many and grievous complaints
against Paul, which they could not
prove.

8 While he answered for himself, Neither against the law of the
Jews, neither against the temple,
nor yet against Caesar, have I
offended any thing at all.

9 But Festus, willing to do the
Jews a pleasure, answered Paul,
and said, Wilt thou go up to
Jerusalem, and there be judged of
these things before me?

10 Then said Paul, I stand at Caesar's judgment seat, where I ought to be judged: to the Jews have I done no wrong, as thou very well knowest.

11 For if I be an offender, or have committed any thing worthy of death, I refuse not to die: but if there be none of these things whereof these accuse me, no man may deliver me unto them. I appeal unto Caesar.

12 Then Festus, when he had conferred with the council, answered, Hast thou appealed unto Caesar? unto Caesar shalt thou go.

13 And after certain days king Agrippa and Bernice came unto Caesarea to salute Festus.

14 And when they had been there many days, Festus declared Paul's cause unto the king, saying, There is a certain man left in bonds by Felix:

15 About whom, when I was at Jerusalem, the chief priests and the elders of the Jews informed me, desiring to have judgment against him.

16 To whom I answered, It is not the manner of the Romans to deliver any man to die, before that he which is accused have the accus-

Notes:

ers face to face, and have licence to answer for himself concerning the crime laid against him.

17 Therefore, when they were come hither, without any delay on the morrow I sat on the judgment seat, and commanded the man to be brought forth.

18 Against whom when the accusers stood up, they brought none accusation of such things as I supposed:

19 But had certain questions against him of their own superstition, and of one Jesus, which was dead, whom Paul affirmed to be alive.

20 And because I doubted of such manner of questions, I asked him whether he would go to Jerusalem, and there be judged of these matters.

21 But when Paul had appealed to be reserved unto the hearing of Augustus, I commanded him to be kept till I might send him to Caesar.

22 Then Agrippa said unto Festus, I would also hear the man myself. To morrow, said he, thou shalt hear him.

23 And on the morrow, when Agrippa was come, and Bernice, with great pomp, and was entered

Notes:

into the place of hearing, with the chief captains, and principal men of the city, at Festus' commandment Paul was brought forth.

24 And Festus said, King Agrippa, and all men which are here present with us, ye see this man, about whom all the multitude of the Jews have dealt with me, both at Jerusalem, and also here, crying that he ought not to live any longer.

25 But when I found that he had committed nothing worthy of death, and that he himself hath appealed to Augustus, I have determined to send him.

26 Of whom I have no certain thing to write unto my lord. Wherefore I have brought him forth before you, and specially before thee, O king Agrippa, that, after examination had, I might have somewhat to write.

27 For it seemeth to me unreasonable to send a prisoner, and not withal to signify the crimes laid against him.

Acts Chapter 26

1 Then Agrippa said unto Paul, Thou art permitted to speak for thyself. Then Paul stretched forth the hand, and answered for himself:

2 I think myself happy, king Agrippa, because I shall answer for myself this day before thee touching all the things whereof I am accused of the Jews:

3 Especially because I know thee to be expert in all customs and questions which are among the Jews: wherefore I beseech thee to hear me patiently.

4 My manner of life from my youth, which was at the first among mine own nation at Jerusalem, know all the Jews;

5 Which knew me from the beginning, if they would testify, that after the most straitest sect of our religion I lived a Pharisee.

6 And now I stand and am judged for the hope of the promise made of God unto our fathers:

7 Unto which promise our twelve tribes, instantly serving God day and night, hope to come. For which hope's sake, king Agrippa, I am accused of the Jews.

8 Why should it be thought a thing incredible with you, that God should raise the dead?

9 I verily thought with myself, that I ought to do many things con-

Notes:

trary to the name of Jesus of Nazareth.

10 Which thing I also did in Jerusalem: and many of the saints did I shut up in prison, having received authority from the chief priests; and when they were put to death, I gave my voice against them.

11 And I punished them oft in every synagogue, and compelled them to blaspheme; and being exceedingly mad against them, I persecuted them even unto strange cities.

12 Whereupon as I went to Damascus with authority and com-mission from the chief priests,

13 At midday, O king, I saw in the way a light from heaven, above the brightness of the sun, shining round about me and them which journeyed with me.

14 And when we were all fallen to the earth, I heard a voice speak-ing unto me, and saying in the Hebrew tongue, Saul, Saul, why persecutest thou me? it is hard for thee to kick against the pricks.

15 And I said, Who art thou, Lord? And he said, I am Jesus whom thou persecutest.

16 But rise, and stand upon thy

Notes:

feet: for I have appeared unto thee for this purpose, to make thee a minister and a witness both of these things which thou hast seen, and of those things in the which I will appear unto thee;

17 Delivering thee from the people, and from the Gentiles, unto whom now I send thee,

18 To open their eyes, and to turn them from darkness to light, and from the power of Satan unto God, that they may receive forgiveness of sins, and inheritance among them which are sanctified by faith that is in me.

19 Whereupon, O king Agrippa, I was not disobedient unto the heavenly vision:

20 But shewed first unto them of Damascus, and at Jerusalem, and throughout all the coasts of Judaea, and then to the Gentiles, that they should repent and turn to God, and do works meet for repentance.

21 For these causes the Jews caught me in the temple, and went about to kill me.

22 Having therefore obtained help of God, I continue unto this day, witnessing both to small and great, saying none other things than those which the prophets and

Moses did say should come:

23 That Christ should suffer, and that he should be the first that should rise from the dead, and should shew light unto the people, and to the Gentiles.

24 And as he thus spake for himself, Festus said with a loud voice, Paul, thou art beside thyself; much learning doth make thee mad.

25 But he said, I am not mad, most noble Festus; but speak forth the words of truth and soberness.

26 For the king knoweth of these things, before whom also I speak freely: for I am persuaded that none of these things are hidden from him; for this thing was not done in a corner.

27 King Agrippa, believest thou the prophets? I know that thou believest.

28 Then Agrippa said unto Paul, Almost thou persuadest me to be a Christian.

29 And Paul said, I would to God, that not only thou, but also all that hear me this day, were both almost, and altogether such as I am, except these bonds.

30 And when he had thus spoken, the king rose up, and the gov-

Notes:

26:28: How sad to be "almost persuaded" yet lost to eternal damnation. Are you "almost persuaded" of the need to (1) repent, (2) be baptized in Jesus name, (3) receive the gift of the Holy Ghost (with the evidence of speaking in other tongues)?

ernor, and Bernice, and they that sat with them:

31 And when they were gone aside, they talked between themselves, saying, This man doeth nothing worthy of death or of bonds.

32 Then said Agrippa unto Festus, This man might have been set at liberty, if he had not appealed unto Caesar.

Acts Chapter 27

1 And when it was determined that we should sail into Italy, they delivered Paul and certain other prisoners unto one named Julius, a centurion of Augustus' band.

2 And entering into a ship of Adramyttium, we launched, meaning to sail by the coasts of Asia; one Aristarchus, a Macedonian of Thessalonica, being with us.

3 And the next day we touched at Sidon. And Julius courteously entreated Paul, and gave him liberty to go unto his friends to refresh himself.

4 And when we had launched from thence, we sailed under Cyprus, because the winds were contrary.

5 And when we had sailed over

Notes:

the sea of Cilicia and Pamphylia, we came to Myra, a city of Lycia.

6 And there the centurion found a ship of Alexandria sailing into Italy; and he put us therein.

7 And when we had sailed slowly many days, and scarce were come over against Cnidus, the wind not suffering us, we sailed under Crete, over against Salmone;

8 And, hardly passing it, came unto a place which is called The fair havens; nigh whereunto was the city of Lasea.

9 Now when much time was spent, and when sailing was now dangerous, because the fast was now already past, Paul admonished them,

10 And said unto them, Sirs, I perceive that this voyage will be with hurt and much damage, not only of the lading and ship, but also of our lives.

11 Nevertheless the centurion believed the master and the owner of the ship, more than those things which were spoken by Paul.

12 And because the haven was not commodious to winter in, the more part advised to depart thence also, if by any means they might attain to Phenice, and there to win-

Notes:

ter; which is an haven of Crete, and lieth toward the south west and north west.

13 And when the south wind blew softly, supposing that they had obtained their purpose, loosing thence, they sailed close by Crete.

14 But not long after there arose against it a tempestuous wind, called Euroclydon.

15 And when the ship was caught, and could not bear up into the wind, we let her drive.

16 And running under a certain island which is called Clauda, we had much work to come by the boat:

17 Which when they had taken up, they used helps, undergirding the ship; and, fearing lest they should fall into the quicksands, strake sail, and so were driven.

18 And we being exceedingly tossed with a tempest, the next day they lightened the ship;

19 And the third day we cast out with our own hands the tackling of the ship.

20 And when neither sun nor stars in many days appeared, and no small tempest lay on us, all hope that we should be saved was then taken away.

21 But after long abstinence Paul stood forth in the midst of them, and said, Sirs, ye should have hearkened unto me, and not have loosed from Crete, and to have gained this harm and loss.

22 And now I exhort you to be of good cheer: for there shall be no loss of any man's life among you, but of the ship.

23 For there stood by me this night the angel of God, whose I am, and whom I serve,

24 Saying, Fear not, Paul; thou must be brought before Caesar: and, lo, God hath given thee all them that sail with thee.

25 Wherefore, sirs, be of good cheer: for I believe God, that it shall be even as it was told me.

26 Howbeit we must be cast upon a certain island.

27 But when the fourteenth night was come, as we were driven up and down in Adria, about midnight the shipmen deemed that they drew near to some country;

28 And sounded, and found it twenty fathoms: and when they had gone a little further, they sounded again, and found it fifteen fathoms.

29 Then fearing lest we should

Notes:

Notes:

have fallen upon rocks, they cast four anchors out of the stern, and wished for the day.

30 And as the shipmen were about to flee out of the ship, when they had let down the boat into the sea, under colour as though they would have cast anchors out of the foreship,

31 Paul said to the centurion and to the soldiers, Except these abide in the ship, ye cannot be saved.

32 Then the soldiers cut off the ropes of the boat, and let her fall off.

33 And while the day was coming on, Paul besought them all to take meat, saying, This day is the fourteenth day that ye have tarried and continued fasting, having taken nothing.

34 Wherefore I pray you to take some meat: for this is for your health: for there shall not an hair fall from the head of any of you.

35 And when he had thus spoken, he took bread, and gave thanks to God in presence of them all: and when he had broken it, he began to eat.

36 Then were they all of good cheer, and they also took some meat.

Notes:

37 And we were in all in the ship two hundred threescore and sixteen souls.

38 And when they had eaten enough, they lightened the ship, and cast out the wheat into the sea.

39 And when it was day, they knew not the land: but they discovered a certain creek with a shore, into the which they were minded, if it were possible, to thrust in the ship.

40 And when they had taken up the anchors, they committed themselves unto the sea, and loosed the rudder bands, and hoised up the mainsail to the wind, and made toward shore.

41 And falling into a place where two seas met, they ran the ship aground; and the forepart stuck fast, and remained unmoveable, but the hinder part was broken with the violence of the waves.

42 And the soldiers' counsel was to kill the prisoners, lest any of them should swim out, and escape.

43 But the centurion, willing to save Paul, kept them from their purpose; and commanded that they which could swim should cast themselves first into the sea, and get to land:

44 And the rest, some on boards, and some on broken pieces of the ship. And so it came to pass, that they escaped all safe to land.

Acts Chapter 28

1 And when they were escaped, then they knew that the island was called Melita.

2 And the barbarous people shewed us no little kindness: for they kindled a fire, and received us every one, because of the present rain, and because of the cold.

3 And when Paul had gathered a bundle of sticks, and laid them on the fire, there came a viper out of the heat, and fastened on his hand.

4 And when the barbarians saw the venomous beast hang on his hand, they said among themselves, No doubt this man is a murderer, whom, though he hath escaped the sea, yet vengeance suffereth not to live.

5 And he shook off the beast into the fire, and felt no harm.

6 Howbeit they looked when he should have swollen, or fallen down dead suddenly: but after they had looked a great while, and saw no harm come to him, they changed their minds, and said that he was a god.

7 In the same quarters were possessions of the chief man of the island, whose name was Publius; who received us, and lodged us three days courteously.

8 And it came to pass, that the father of Publius lay sick of a fever and of a bloody flux: to whom Paul entered in, and prayed, and laid his hands on him, and healed him.

9 So when this was done, others also, which had diseases in the island, came, and were healed:

10 Who also honoured us with many honours; and when we departed, they laded us with such things as were necessary.

11 And after three months we departed in a ship of Alexandria, which had wintered in the isle, whose sign was Castor and Pollux.

12 And landing at Syracuse, we tarried there three days.

13 And from thence we fetched a compass, and came to Rhegium: and after one day the south wind blew, and we came the next day to Puteoli:

14 Where we found brethren, and were desired to tarry with them seven days: and so we went toward Rome.

15 And from thence, when the

Notes:

brethren heard of us, they came to meet us as far as Appiiforum, and The three taverns: whom when Paul saw, he thanked God, and took courage.

16 And when we came to Rome, the centurion delivered the prisoners to the captain of the guard: but Paul was suffered to dwell by himself with a soldier that kept him.

17 And it came to pass, that after three days Paul called the chief of the Jews together: and when they were come together, he said unto them, Men and brethren, though I have committed nothing against the people, or customs of our fathers, yet was I delivered prisoner from Jerusalem into the hands of the Romans.

18 Who, when they had examined me, would have let me go, because there was no cause of death in me.

19 But when the Jews spake against it, I was constrained to appeal unto Caesar; not that I had ought to accuse my nation of.

20 For this cause therefore have I called for you, to see you, and to speak with you: because that for the hope of Israel I am bound with this chain.

Notes:

21 And they said unto him, We neither received letters out of Judaea concerning thee, neither any of the brethren that came shewed or spake any harm of thee.

22 But we desire to hear of thee what thou thinkest: for as concerning this sect, we know that every where it is spoken against.

23 And when they had appointed him a day, there came many to him into his lodging; to whom he expounded and testified the kingdom of God, persuading them concerning Jesus, both out of the law of Moses, and out of the prophets, from morning till evening.

24 And some believed the things which were spoken, and some believed not.

25 And when they agreed not among themselves, they departed, after that Paul had spoken one word, Well spake the Holy Ghost by Esaias the prophet unto our fathers,

26 Saying, Go unto this people, and say, Hearing ye shall hear, and shall not understand; and seeing ye shall see, and not perceive:

27 For the heart of this people is waxed gross, and their ears are dull of hearing, and their eyes have they

Notes:

closed; lest they should see with their eyes, and hear with their ears, and understand with their heart, and should be converted, and I should heal them.

28 Be it known therefore unto you, that the salvation of God is sent unto the Gentiles, and that they will hear it.

29 And when he had said these words, the Jews departed, and had great reasoning among themselves.

30 And Paul dwelt two whole years in his own hired house, and received all that came in unto him,

31 Preaching the kingdom of God, and teaching those things which concern the Lord Jesus Christ, with all confidence, no man forbidding him.

Section 3
Getting the Full Benefit

Our Need of Salvation

Due to the original sin of Adam (back in the beginning) we are all born with a sinful nature. Sin (any behavior contrary to the law of God) separates us from God. Sin is harmful to us in many ways — emotionally, physically and spiritually. **Salvation** refers to God redeeming a person, washing away their sins, and bringing him or her into God's community (the church) and into communion with God for **eternal life**.

- "But God commendeth his love toward us, in that, while we were yet sinners, Christ died for us" (Romans 5:8).
- "For as by one man's disobedience many were made sinners, so by the obedience of one shall many be made righteous" (Romans 5:19).
- "They that are whole have no need of the physician, but they that are sick: I came not to call the righteous, but sinners to repentance" (Mark 2:17).

God's Plan for Our Salvation: New Birth

The **gospel** of Jesus Christ can be simply summarized as the death, burial, and resurrection of Jesus. The sinless Son of God died

for the sins of all those who would dare to
believe. He was buried in a borrowed tomb,
and He was resurrected after three days
and three nights in the grave. Now the key
question is: *What shall we do (to respond
to the gospel of Jesus Christ)?* **The answer
is to be** *born again.*

Jesus said, "Verily, verily, I say unto thee,
except a man be **born again**, he cannot see
the kingdom of God" (John 3:3). Jesus then
explained what this new birth is: "Verily,
verily, I say unto thee, except a man be born
of **water** and of the **Spirit**, he cannot enter
into the kingdom of God" (John 3:5).

Jesus also taught that repentance is necessary, and that repentance and remission of
sins would be preached in His name:

- "Then opened he their understanding,
  that they might understand the scriptures, and said unto them, Thus it is
  written, and thus it behoved Christ to
  suffer, and to rise from the dead the
  third day: And that repentance and
  remission of sins should be preached in
  his name among all nations, beginning
  at Jerusalem" (Luke 24:45-47).
- "Bring forth therefore fruits meet for
  repentance" (Matthew 3:8).

- "From that time Jesus began to preach, and to say, Repent: for the kingdom of heaven is at hand" (Matthew 4:17).

Thus the Bible reveals God's plan for our salvation, in which God, the church, and the believer all act in concert. Being born again involves three simple steps of faith. Each step identifies us with Jesus and His gospel:

Repentance
Repentance is an act of faith on the part of a new believer, in which one turns away from sin and toward God. Your previous time as a sinner (the old man) dies, and your new life of righteousness begins. This identifies with Jesus' death on the cross.

Water Baptism in Jesus Name
Proper baptism — being immersed in water with the name of Jesus invoked aloud — is an essential step in becoming a Christian. After Jesus was crucified, His followers buried Him in a borrowed tomb. Once a believer has repented — become dead to sin — he is to bury the old lifestyle through water baptism. This identifies us with the burial of Jesus. The Bible says, "We are buried with him [Jesus] by baptism" (Romans 6:4). Baptism is an act of faith on the part of both the church and the believer.

The Gift of the Holy Ghost

God is a Spirit (John 4:24), and He is holy (righteous, without sin). Thus the Bible often refers to God by the terms Holy Ghost and Holy Spirit. The most amazing fact of biblical salvation is that a person can go from being a sinner (separated from God) to being a Christian—so unified with God that His Spirit dwells inside the believer! No one can adequately describe this; it must be experienced. Because of the power of God dwelling inside, a Spirit-filled believer can live in a realm previously unattainable. God's Spirit provides the power to live a new life and thus identifies with the resurrection of Jesus. It is an act of God upon the believer who receives, through faith, the gift promised in the Word of God, evidenced by speaking with other tongues.

EXPERIENCE THE NEW BIRTH TODAY!

OBEY ACTS 2:38!

After having read the Book of Acts, with the comments presented to help highlight both some important points and a brief history of the formation of several of the first century churches, one can see that every believer's baptism recorded in the first century churches was done in the name of Jesus.

You may have some questions at this point. We want to spend the next few paragraphs answering some common questions, such as:

* Is water baptism truly essential?
* What about the Matthew 28:19 verse?
* What if a prior water baptism was in three titles and not in Jesus name?
* What about sprinkling or pouring?
* What if one was baptized as an infant?
* And more...

Helpful Information on Water Baptism
After repentance, the next step of obedient faith for any newly believing Christian is water baptism in the name of Jesus. The word *baptize* comes from the Greek word *baptizo* which means to immerse or dunk. After Jesus was crucified on the cross, He was buried in a tomb, where He lay until His resurrection three days & nights later. The Scriptures clearly reveal that Christian believers are to become identified with the Lord's burial by being baptized. Practically speaking, water baptism is an act of faith in which each believer is buried momentarily in water while having the name of Jesus invoked aloud. Scriptures also reveal a connection between water baptism and our

spiritual cleansing (from sin) for the salvation of the believer. Thus, water baptism has two distinct meanings:

Washing (or cleansing):

- "Then went out to him Jerusalem, and all Judea, and all the region round about Jordan, and were baptized of him in Jordan, confessing their sins" (Matthew 3:5-6).

Burial with Christ:

- "Therefore we are buried with him by baptism into death: that like as Christ was raised up from the dead by the glory of the Father, even so we also should walk in newness of life" (Romans 6:4).

- "In whom also ye are circumcised with the circumcision made without hands, in putting off the body of the sins of the flesh by the circumcision of Christ: buried with him in baptism, wherein also ye are risen with him through the faith of the operation of God, who hath raised him from the dead" (Colossians 2:11-12).

Old Testament Typology:

During the great flood, Noah and his family were saved by water. So also we are saved by water baptism during the church age:

- "The longsuffering of God waited in the days of Noah, while the ark was a preparing, wherein few, that is, eight souls were saved by water. **The like figure whereunto even baptism doth also now save us** (not the putting away of the filth of the flesh, but the answer of a good conscience toward God,) by the resurrection of Jesus Christ" (I Peter 3:20-21).

Just as the Hebrews were saved by water while passing through the Red Sea (to escape from Pharaoh's armies), so also we are saved by water baptism:

- "Moreover, brethren, I would not that ye should be ignorant, how that all our fathers were under the cloud, and all passed through the sea; and were all baptized unto Moses in the cloud and in the sea; and did all eat the same spiritual meat; and did all drink the same spiritual drink: for they drank of that spiritual Rock that followed them: and that Rock was Christ" (I Corinthians 10:1-4).

The early church (the first-century church led by the Apostles) fulfilled the command of Jesus regarding water baptism:

- "Then Peter said unto them, Repent, and be baptized every one of you in the name of Jesus Christ for the remission of sins, and ye shall receive the gift of the Holy Ghost" (Acts 2:38).
- "They were baptized in the name of the Lord Jesus" (Acts 8:16).
- "And he commanded them to be baptized in the name of the Lord" (Acts 10:48a).
- "When they heard this, they were baptized in the name of the Lord Jesus" (Acts 19:5).

How were believers baptized during the time of the Apostles? According to the Bible, believers were baptized by immersion in water, with the name of Jesus invoked aloud over each believer during the event.

Immersion in water:

- "And John also was baptizing in Aenon near to Salim, because there was much water there: and they came, and were baptized" (John 3:23).

- "And he commanded the chariot to stand still: and they went down both into the water, both Philip and the eunuch; and he baptized him. And when they were come up out of the water, the Spirit of the Lord caught away Philip, that the eunuch saw him no more: and he went on his way rejoicing" (Acts 8:38-39).

What about sprinkling or pouring? What if one was baptized as an infant?

We simply do not find these practices in the Scriptures. Neither sprinkling, nor pouring, nor infant baptism can be found or substantiated in the Word of God. These are human traditions; therefore we should reject them in the light of scriptural truth. The Bible says that water baptism is "the answer of a good conscience toward God" (I Peter 3:20-21). Since infants are not old enough to comprehend the gospel, they cannot conscientiously decide to be baptized. While infants may be blessed and dedicated to God through prayer, they must still be baptized when they are old enough.

In the Scriptures, what formula was used in baptism? In whose name were they baptized? Does it matter?

Prior to the birth of the church, the prophet John (called John the Baptist) baptized many followers in Judea. The Bible does not mention John using anyone's name during his baptisms, saying only that John baptized unto repentance. However, after the death of Jesus and with the birth of the church (you read about it in Acts, chapter 2) water baptism was updated; the Lord's name was added to it. The greatest legacy the Lord left to His bride (the church) is His name!

+ "Neither is there salvation in any other: for there is none other name under heaven given among men, whereby we must be saved" (Acts 4:12).

In the New Testament, the name of Jesus was invoked aloud over each believer during water baptism. No other baptismal mode was ever practiced in the church during the time of the apostles:

+ "Then Peter said unto them, Repent, and be baptized every one of you in the name of Jesus Christ for the remission of sins, and ye shall receive the gift of the Holy Ghost" (Acts 2:38).
+ "They were baptized in the name of the Lord Jesus" (Acts 8:16).
+ "And he commanded them to be bap-

tized in the name of the Lord" (Acts 10:48a).

+ "When they heard this, they were baptized in the name of the Lord Jesus" (Acts 19:5).

Other pertinent verses:

+ "Know ye not, that so many of us as were baptized into Jesus Christ were baptized into his death?" (Romans 6:3).
+ "And whatsoever ye do in word or deed, do all in the name of the Lord Jesus, giving thanks to God and the Father by him" (Colossians 3:17).

Jesus' name must be invoked verbally in order to have a proper baptism! Notice the questions Paul the Apostle asked the church at Corinth:

+ "Is Christ divided? Was Paul crucified for you? Or were ye baptized in the name of Paul?" (I Corinthians 1:13).

Since Jesus is the one who was crucified for us, we should be baptized in His name! Look at Paul's own baptism (see Acts 22:16):

+ "And now why tarriest thou? arise, and be baptized, and wash away thy sins, calling on the name of the Lord."

Does water baptism matter? Water baptism is a command to be obeyed for salvation!

- "And he commanded them to be baptized in the name of the Lord" (Acts 10:48).
- "And he said unto them, Go ye into all the world, and preach the gospel to every creature. He that believeth and is baptized shall be saved; but he that believeth not shall be damned" (Mark 16:15-16).
- "For as many of you as have been baptized into Christ have put on Christ" (Galatians 3:27).
- "Then they that gladly received his word were baptized: and the same day there were added unto them about three thousand souls" (Acts 2:41).
- "One Lord, one faith, one baptism" (Ephesians 4:5).

What about Matthew 28:19? Some use this verse to support a baptismal formula that does not include the name of Jesus. Let's examine it closely:

- "Go ye therefore, and teach all nations, baptizing them in the name of the Father, and of the Son, and of the Holy Ghost" (Matthew 28:19).

There are only two ways to act upon this verse (and only one way is correct). Either we are to repeat these words when we baptize, or we are to obey these words, baptizing in a singular name. Notice in the verse above that "the name" is singular. This verse does not say "names."

When Jesus spoke the words of Matthew 28:19, He was speaking to His Apostles. It is apparent that His Apostles did not interpret the words as a formula to be repeated. Any study of the New Testament shows that the Apostles obeyed this verse rather than repeating the words. The New Testament clearly confirms that believers were baptized in the name of Jesus.

To truly obey Matthew 28:19, one must discover the singular "name" of the Father, and of the Son, and of the Holy Ghost. That singular name is Jesus.

Matthew 28:19 was obeyed in the Book of Acts, through baptism in the name of Jesus. We should obey this verse today, by being baptized in the name of Jesus.

The Book of Acts is the *only* book in the Bible where New Covenant water baptisms are recorded after Jesus' resurrection. The

Apostles had walked with Jesus, and He had opened their understanding (see Luke 24:45-47). They baptized using Jesus name and not the "titles" (Father, Son and Holy Ghost). Since God gave us the Bible to "study to show ourselves approved"and there are no examples of baptisms occurring in any other manner after Jesus' resurrection, it is obvious that man later changed the form of baptism from that which God wanted (*in the name of Jesus*) to something else (*in the name of the Father, and of the Son and of the Holy Ghost*). Should we baptize according to the manner God instituted or in the manner instituted by man? "Let God be true, but every man a liar" (Romans 3:4).

If you were previously baptized by the preacher saying, "in the name of the Father and of the Son and of the Holy Ghost" then the name of Jesus was not used, and by all indications you need to be rebaptized! The only New Covenant baptism known to be biblically valid is to use the name of Jesus. In Colossians 3:17, Paul instructed the church saying, "and whatsoever ye do in word or deed, **do all** in the name of the Lord Jesus." We pray over food in the name of Jesus. We pray for healing in the name of Jesus. We pray for God's intervention in our lives in the name of Jesus. Why, then, do we not **do all** and baptize in the name of Jesus?

Receiving the Gift of the Holy Ghost
Once you repent and commit to being water baptized in the name of Jesus, you're ready for the wonderful gift of the Holy Spirit!

Old Testament prophecy:

+ "A new heart also will I give you, and a new spirit will I put within you: and I will take away the stony heart out of your flesh, and I will give you an heart of flesh. And I will put my spirit within you, and cause you to walk in my statutes, and ye shall keep my judgments, and do them" (Ezekiel 36:26-27).
+ "And it shall come to pass afterward, that I will pour out my spirit upon all flesh; and your sons and your daughters shall prophesy, your old men shall dream dreams, your young men shall see visions" (Joel 2:28).

Jesus prophesied of the outpouring of the Spirit:

+ "He that believeth on me, as the scripture hath said, out of his belly shall flow rivers of living water. (But this spake he of the Spirit, which they that believe on

him should receive: for the Holy Ghost
was not yet given; because that Jesus
was not yet glorified)" (John 7:38-39).

Notice that Jesus' words (above) illustrate
that all believers should receive the Holy
Spirit! Also note the first baptism of the
Holy Ghost (the birthday of the church):

- "And when the day of Pentecost was
  fully come, they were all with one
  accord in one place. And suddenly
  there came a sound from heaven as of a
  rushing mighty wind, and it filled all
  the house where they were sitting. And
  there appeared unto them cloven
  tongues like as of fire, and it sat upon
  each of them. And they were all filled
  with the Holy Ghost, and began to
  speak with other tongues, as the Spirit
  gave them utterance" (Acts 2:1-4).

Contrary to the teaching of some, one does
not automatically receive the gift of the
Holy Ghost at the moment he believes.
Receiving the gift of the Spirit is a separate,
dynamic experience that is part of the new
birth! Consider receiving the Holy Ghost as
you read the following passage of Scripture:

- "Then Philip went down to the city of

Samaria, and preached Christ unto them. . . . And the people with one accord gave heed unto those things which Philip spake, hearing and seeing the miracles which he did. . . . and there was great joy in that city . . . But when they believed Philip preaching the things concerning the kingdom of God, and the name of Jesus Christ, they were baptized, both men and women. . . . Now when the apostles which were at Jerusalem heard that Samaria had received the word of God, they sent unto them Peter and John: who, when they were come down, prayed for them, that they might receive the Holy Ghost: (For as yet he was fallen upon none of them; only they were baptized in the name of the Lord Jesus.) . . . . Then laid they their hands on them, and they received the Holy Ghost" (Acts 8:5-17).

In the passage below, the Scriptures reveal that "believing" is a separate event from water baptism and from the experience of receiving the Holy Ghost.

* "Paul . . . came to Ephesus: and finding certain disciples, he said unto them, Have ye received the Holy Ghost since ye believed? And they said unto him,

We have not so much as heard whether there be any Holy Ghost. And he said unto them, Unto what then were ye baptized? And they said, Unto John's baptism. Then said Paul, John verily baptized with the baptism of repentance, saying unto the people, that they should believe on him which should come after him, that is, on Christ Jesus. When they heard this, they were baptized in the name of the Lord Jesus. And when Paul had laid his hands upon them, the Holy Ghost came on them; and they spake with tongues, and prophesied" (Acts 19:1-6).

Is the baptism of the Holy Ghost necessary for salvation?

- "Jesus said, Verily, verily, I say unto thee, Except a man be born again, he cannot see the kingdom of God" (John 3:3).

Jesus then explained what this new birth is:

- "Verily, verily, I say unto thee, except a man be born of water and of the Spirit, he cannot enter into the kingdom of God" (John 3:5).

Both water and the Spirit are necessary for

the new birth and to enter into the kingdom of God!

The Holy Ghost experience described in the Book of Acts is part of the new birth!

- "In whom ye also trusted, after that ye heard the word of truth, the gospel of your salvation: in whom also after that ye believed, ye were sealed with that holy Spirit of promise" (Ephesians 1:13).

Some ask honestly, "But will not my church attendance and my being a good person save me?" The answer is no. We all must be born again. If any man could have been saved by his own works, it would be the righteous Cornelius of Caesarea (described in the tenth chapter of Acts). But even that pious man had to be born again:

- "There was a certain man in Caesarea called Cornelius . . . . a devout man, and one that feared God with all his house, which gave much alms to the people, and prayed to God alway. He saw in a vision . . . an angel of God coming in to him, and saying unto him, Cornelius . . . Thy prayers and thine alms are come up for a memorial before God . . . . And

now send men to Joppa, and call for
Peter . . . he shall tell thee what thou
oughtest to do" (Acts 10:1-6).

Cornelius called for Peter, who came and
preached to Cornelius and his entire household. God poured out His Spirit upon them
all, and Peter commanded them to be baptized in the name of the Lord.

Good works is not enough. Being devout is
not enough to save you. You must seek
truth. Update your spirituality! We all must
be born again!

Tongues: Sign of the Gift of the Holy Spirit
The single common sign of the baptism of
the Holy Ghost is speaking in tongues as
the Spirit gives the utterance.

Old Testament prophecy:

   ◆ "For with stammering lips and another
     tongue will he speak to this people"
     (Isaiah 28:11).

New Testament evidence:

   ◆ Acts 2:4, Acts 10:45-46, and Acts 19:6 all
     mention tongues as the sign of receiv-
     ing the Holy Ghost.

Speaking with tongues as God's Spirit gives

the utterance is the initial, physical sign of the Holy Spirit baptism. While this is not the only sign, it is an immediately noticeable, miraculous sign of having received the gift of the Holy Spirit.

Have you received the Holy Ghost since you believed? Have you been water baptized in Jesus' name?

Life magazine has noted that the Pentecostal phenomenon of receiving the Holy Ghost and speaking with tongues is one of the most significant events of the last hundred years. Millions upon millions of people worldwide have now been born again according to God's Word. Have you?

The promise of real freedom awaits you:

 • "For the promise is unto you, and to your children, and to all that are afar off, even as many as the Lord our God shall call" (Acts 2:39).

Summary

Man has twisted scriptures since the time of Christ, out of ignorance or to make them fit personal beliefs. Yet the Lord changes not (see Malachi 3:6 and Hebrews 13:8). His Word will stand forever (see Isaiah 40:8 and I Peter 1:25)! The most damning changes that men have implemented are those concerning salvation, the topic to which this book is devoted. Below are some examples of false doctrine:

The Romans Road [to salvation] teaches essentially that, "If you believe in Jesus, you're saved" — supposedly neither water baptism nor Spirit baptism are needed.

- Salvation in the Romans Road doctrine is based on Romans 10:9 which states, "That if thou shalt confess with thy mouth the Lord Jesus, and shalt believe in thine heart that God hath raised him from the dead, thou shalt be saved."
- The Epistle to the Romans was not addressed to lost souls. It was addressed to previously-converted members of the church in Rome (Romans 1:7). They had already been baptized in Jesus name and had been filled with the Holy Ghost evidenced by speaking in other tongues as the Apostles taught (as pointed out and discussed throughout the preceding Bible study).
- Romans was not written in a void, and should not be viewed as isolated away from Acts 2:38, nor used as a means to nullify Acts 2:38, which tells lost souls three essential steps to obey in faith.

False teachers say that you don't have to be baptized in water because "the thief on the cross wasn't baptized, and he was saved."

- The Church Age didn't begin until the Feast of Pentecost that is recorded in the Book of Acts. This was 50 days after Jesus' crucifixion.
- The Apostle Paul revealed that we are to be baptized in the name of the One who crucified for us (see I Corinthians 1:13). Prior to Jesus' death on the cross, baptism in His name was not yet in force because He had not yet died for us.
- The Lord Jesus taught and stressed the importance of water baptism. He submitted Himself to be baptized, and He gave full understanding to His Apostles, who later commanded water baptism. The fact that Jesus (prior to His death) granted salvation to a man who was about to die and had no access to water baptism, does not mean we can or should circumvent a biblical command!
- On that Day of Pentecost in Acts 2, everything changed concerning salvation. From then until the day that the Lord returns for His church, the plan of salvation in Acts 2:38 will be what we are judged by, concerning our accept-

ance of Christ. We are accountable to the Bible standard for full salvation:

(1) repentance from sin,
(2) water baptism in Jesus name by full immersion, and
(3) receiving the gift of the Holy Ghost evidenced by speaking in another tongue (language).

All of this was discussed previously within <u>The Book of Salvation</u>.

False teachers say that whenever you accept Christ as your personal savior, you silently and automatically receive the baptism of the Holy Ghost.

- Acts 8:16 clearly refutes that argument. See the comments beside that scripture verse within this Bible study (page 58).

False teachers say that when you pray the "Sinner's Prayer," you are saved if you prayed it with sincerity — supposedly water baptism and Spirit baptism aren't needed.

- Although it is a good first step, you are not saved until you obey from the heart the plan of salvation in Acts 2:38. According to the Lord Jesus, one must be born of the **water** and of the **Spirit** (John 3:5).

False teachers claim that we should water baptize converts by saying "in the name of the Father, and of the Son and of the Holy Ghost" — like Jesus said in Matthew 28:19. Yet Jesus is the only name that qualifies!

+ What is the name of the Son? *Jesus*. And note that His name also qualifies as that of the Father and the Holy Ghost:

+ What is the name of the Father? Since Jesus came in His Father's name (John 5:43), and since the Father and Son (Jesus) are one (John 10:30), and since it was prophesied that the Lord's name is to be one (Zechariah 14:9), and since the Son's name is Jesus (Matthew 1:21), and since God the Father is glorified when we worship Jesus by bowing to Him and confessing Jesus Christ as Lord (Philippians 2:11), then we should recognize that by calling upon the name of Jesus we have access to God the Father, and that, for those of us alive in the New Covenant, Jesus is the person and name by which God the Father desires to be addressed and accessed.

+ What is the name of the Holy Ghost? The terms Spirit and Ghost are synonymous. The Bible says, "God is a Spirit" (John 4:24). There is every reason to hold that all the prior points, about the name of the Father, should apply. But there is more. Since there is only one Spirit (Ephesians 4:4), and since there is only one Lord (Ephesians 4:5), and since Jesus is the Lord (Philippians 2:11), and since the Word of the Lord says, "the Lord is that Spirit" (II Corinthians 3:17), and since, while He was describing the Holy Spirit's arrival to dwell within believers, Jesus Christ said, "I will not leave you comfortless, I will come unto you" (John 14:18), then we should recognize that the Holy Spirit is "Christ in you, the hope of glory" (Colossians 1:27), and that Christ's redemptive name for all New Covenant believers is Jesus.

- It is apparent that the Apostles, whose understanding had been opened by Jesus, knew that the Lord's words in Matthew 28:19 meant to baptize in Jesus name, because that is what they did! Obviously the Lord meant for us to use His name, not just repeat His titles.

- If you're baptized in the titles and not in the name of Jesus, you should be rebaptized in His name—Jesus! There are no scriptures that show anyone being baptized in the titles. There are many scriptures (as shown in this Bible study) revealing that New Covenant converts were baptized in Jesus name.

Your salvation is dependent on you under-standing and acting on the Word of God — not upon what man teaches, but the Word of God. This Bible study points you to and explains three steps of faith that are essen-tial for conversion unto salvation. Staying saved is a topic for another Bible study.

EXPERIENCE THE NEW BIRTH TODAY!

OBEY ACTS 2:38!

"Then Peter said unto them, Repent, and be baptized every one of you in the name of Jesus Christ for the remission of sins, and ye shall receive the gift of the Holy Ghost" (Acts 2:38).

Visit us online if you have questions, and to get help in locating biker-friendly churches that preach the whole truth of God's word!

---

www.AzusaStreetRiders.com

Azusa StreetRiders

The Apostolic motorcycle ministry of Jesus Christ!

About the Authors

Fred Beall (seen here with his wife, Diane)
is the founder and president of
Azusa StreetRiders, the Apostolic
Motorcycle Ministry of Jesus Christ.
The Bealls make their home in Myrtle Beach, SC.

Doug Joseph is a husband, father of four, and
serves as pastor of Christian Apostolic Church in
Clarksburg, WV as well as president of the
WV Chapter of the Azusa StreetRiders
Apostolic Motorcycle Ministry.
Other books by Doug Joseph include:
"New I.M.mortal" (www.newimmortal.com) and
"Life and Ministry of Billy and Shirley Cole"
as told by the same to Doug and LaDonna Joseph
(www.billycolebook.com)

Made in the USA
Middletown, DE
16 August 2023